CUTTING
Training the Horse and Rider

by Bill Freeman
with Gala Nettles

CUTTING
Training the Horse and Rider

by BILL FREEMAN
with GALA NETTLES

published by

EquiMedia Corporation

CUTTING
TRAINING THE HORSE AND RIDER

Bill Freeman	*Author*
Gala Nettles	*Editor*
Robert Feinberg	*Graphic Designer*
Kathy Kadash	*Photographers*
Rick Swan	
Kelly McMahon	*Illustrator*
Taro Kodama	*Production Asst.*
Marilyn Behrendt	*Proofreader*

Published by EquiMedia Corporation
P.O. Box 90519
Austin, Texas 78709-0519
Tel: 512-288-1676

Printed in Singapore

ISBN: 0-9625898-0-2

I dedicate this book to some very special people in my life: my father, who gave me my foundation in training and showing horses and the opportunity to ride some great horses as a child; my uncle Frederick Dalby, who each summer patiently taught me about cattle and general horsemanship; my wife and children, who have walked with me through the bad times as well as the good ones.

Contents

Preface

BY GALA NETTLES

As cutting horse trainer Buster Welch once stated, "Cutting is either awfully simple or simply awful, depending on your performance for two and a half minutes." What seems so simple to a spectator no doubt took months and months to perfect. Even after such extreme dedication, those fluid movements that appear awfully simple can change with the next performance to movements that are simply awful. This book is a guide to attaining more awfully simple runs than simply awful ones.

Freeman takes you step by step through his training program for cutting horses beginning with the first ride through the first show at least a year later. Although it is basically a program of simple maneuvers—stop, rock back and turn around—it is not simple to explain. And though it may be simple to comprehend, performing the tasks takes work and dedication.

Training a cutting horse Freeman-style is not a package of one technique followed neatly one after another. Instead, it's a program that teaches the 2-year-old the same maneuvers that are used to tune an older horse. The only difference between the lessons for the two horses is in their degree of difficulty. Freeman expects correctness, "cow smarts," and intensity to accompany the repetitious lessons and maturity. The same technique that began at a walk in the beginning of the program ends up as a polished, precision-move in the show arena.

The book falls easily into three sections. Beginning with a section on Freeman's philosophies, horsemanship and a book overview, it continues into a section on the basic training steps and methods for correcting common problems. Here you can learn the techniques for starting the cutting horse as well as the skills to finish him. You learn to recognize mistakes and then how to fix them. The last section offers ideas on show preparation from readying your horse to mentally preparing yourself to studying cattle.

It takes a lot of desire and hours of practice to put these lessons together and build a beautiful run. Even then, you'll still have days with simply awful runs. But, by reading this book, you may have days when your run seems awfully simple.

Profile

When one is born the son of a legendary cutting horse trainer like Shorty Freeman, life automatically revolves around horses. As a young child Bill Freeman, Shorty's son, played cowboys and Indians on the backs of well-bred horses when most children were happily occupied with stick horses. Working arenas substituted as his playground and haystacks and feed bins provided hiding places. Horse conversations continually hovered in the air above Bill and his sister, Sharon, who entertained themselves at the feet of some of the all-time greats in cutting. From the very beginning, the life of Bill Freeman has always been immersed in horses.

"Daddy actually started in the cutting horse business shortly after I was born. His first real cutting horse job was down around Houston. Then he worked a while for Barney Skipper and later we moved to Chilicothe, Texas, where he worked for Oscar Dodson. I was four when we moved to Chilicothe and I'd been riding horses from the time I was two."

Just as horses surrounded Bill's life, so did cutting and training. In fact, under the guidance of his father, Bill received the Shorty Freeman style of training. By the tender age of 4, young Bill was already riding cutting horses, and shortly after that, he had the job of breaking his own horse.

"**Western Horseman Magazine** had a picture of me back then since I was a youngster cutting. But my early experiences with horses were probably a little different than a lot of other kids who start riding horses at a young age.

"Daddy had a great philosophy, and that was 'experience teaches'. That philosophy covered more than just riding a horse. Every year from about the time I was 6, he would give me a horse to break. Now I'm sure he had already done some preliminaries to these horses, but he never told me that, so I felt a great deal of accomplishment at a very young age.

"I also learned to be very independent. I had to figure out everything, including ways to get this horse saddled. I wasn't big enough to throw a saddle, so I learned how to put a rope over the top of a rafter in the barn, hoist the saddle up, walk the horse underneath it and let the saddle down."

Bill's education under the capable eyes of his father filled the days of his youth and horses continued to be his main interest until he became a teen-ager. During those years, Shorty went on the road extensively showing horses, and with his Dad gone from home, Bill's interests slipped from horses to the usual interest of teenage boys — football and girls.

"There weren't a lot of horses around the place when Daddy was gone showing horses. He took them with him. Back then it wasn't a training operation like we have today,

The son of a legendary cutting horse trainer, Bill was already cutting by the early age of four.

so I lost interest and I really never got back into showing for years."

Just before Bill's sophomore year in high school, the Freeman family moved to Graford, Texas, where Shorty did set up his own training operation. There he built a barn, took in horses to train, and although the younger Freeman was once again surrounded by horses and some of the responsibility that went with a training station, his interest in cutting horses did not return.

"I was a typical teen-ager and just not really interested in Daddy's work. I liked the horses, but I preferred roping. Sharon had married Terry Riddle and he was a roper and I liked that. On the weekends I'd go to rodeos with them and ride bulls and bareback horses."

Although Bill graduated from Graford High School, quite a few educational lessons were still to come. The first lesson came that summer. Bill joined the working hands at Boyd Ranch where Shorty and Buster Welch had teamed up. Although cutting was the profession at Boyd Ranch, it wasn't the profession for most of the cow hands, especially the two trainers' sons.

"Buster's son, Greg, and I would rope at night, but we were not working cutting horses! My job at the ranch was looking at cattle and seeding the country by hand on horseback."

The long, hot, monotonous hours of slowly riding across Boyd ranch broadcasting seed made college life look rather appealing, so when September rolled around Bill left behind his ranch education to enroll at Tarleton College.

"I only went to college one year. It was just like the cutting horses; my interest wasn't there either."

At the same time that Bill dropped out of college and went to the oil fields, Shorty remarried and went to Scottsdale, Arizona. For the next several years father and son were apart as the younger Freeman worked in the oil fields during the day and rodeoed on the weekend. Life may have continued along this path had it not been for an intervening car accident which left Bill out of work and on foot.

"Daddy called me one evening to see if I would like some temporary employment. He wanted to fly me to Phoenix where I would pick up a stallion he was hauling, King Skeet, and haul him to Florida to some cuttings. With King Skeet, Daddy was a contender that year for the NCHA World Championship title and needed to make the Florida shows, but he was also training Docs Kitty for the NCHA Futurity and needed to stay home as much as possible. If I hauled King Skeet to Florida, he could fly in, make the shows and fly out. I gladly did it, but the trip was tough pulling that rig straight through from Arizona to Florida and back by myself. But, the good news was when I got back to Phoenix, Daddy had found a permanent job for me."

For the next couple of years, Bill worked in a feed yard in Phoenix. Yet, he still rode bulls and saddle broncs on the weekends. Later, he worked at a ranch where he became intrigued with a young lady named Karen Aberg. Finally, he wandered back to Shorty's Bend End Stables. Once again, cutting began to interest him. For the first time, the younger Freeman began showing cutting horses on his own.

"Sonny Braman had a mare called Heart 109 there, and I was allowed to show her if I paid my own entry fees. This is what really got me started with the cutting horses again."

Bill once again left the tutelage of the elder Freeman, and moved to Cleveland, Ohio, to work for Braman. In the meantime, he and Karen were wed. But employment again came to a halt through another car accident.

"After the NCHA World Finals in Las Vegas that year, we stopped in Phoenix to visit Karen's parents on the way back to Ohio. The day before we were suppose to leave, I had a really bad head-on collision with a van that pulled out in front of me. I was in a convertible pulling a horse trailer. The trailer broke loose and I remember seeing that trailer all around me. When it was finally over, the trailer hit the van head-on and its skid marks were on the trunk of that convertible."

Bill spent the next eight months recuperating from the accident. Since he was unable to work, he, Karen and their 3-year-old daughter Tina lived with Karen's parents in a two-room apartment. Karen's father, Walter Aberg, owned a gasoline station, and five months after the accident, Bill began pumping gas because the doctors wouldn't release him to ride horses.

"Gene Suiter offered me a job but since I wasn't allowed to ride horses, I couldn't take it. But about 30 days after that, I received my medical release and Tom Lyons hired me."

Lyons did his training at night so for the next year, Bill continued pumping gas in the morning. He also started breaking race horses in the afternoon and slept whenever he could. Although Bill credits his father with giving him the gift and talent to train cutting horses, he credits Lyons with teaching him about the business side of cutting.

"Tom was a communicator and he gave me somewhat of a free hand. We had a good rapport. I never felt like I was beneath Tom. I felt like we were a great team. Tom was very successful then, winning the NCHA Derby twice and the NCHA Futurity once, so it was a great period of time for me to learn.

"Between Daddy and Tom, I established my roots in cutting. With the gift of Daddy's talent and by watching him and being able to get on his horses, I learned a lot. Tom gave me the understanding that I needed and taught me the 'why'. Put that with what I learned that summer from Buster, and my own program started to come together. But, I have to credit Daddy with most of it. He gave me the opportunity to learn from a great and to ride greats."

With time, non-professional cutter Bob Sims provided Bill with his first training operation. Sims had a "Freckles" mare at Lyons Training Stables which Freeman really liked, so Lyons allowed him to train the mare.

"I would work her when Bob came to see the mare, so I got to know Bob. Before long, he bought a place in Missouri and offered the place to me to start my own business. Karen and I jumped at the chance."

Karen's "over the hill" gelding, Sims' Freckles mare, and the Freemans moved to Missouri, where they called home for the next seven years. Bill began building a business and his reputation.

"In those early years, it was just me and Karen. We fed, watered, loped, and trained. But, we made a pretty good team."

During the building phase of both his business and his reputation, Walter Hellyer brought horses to Bill to train. "I had a stud for Walter named Guthrie Flit, but we called him Brand X. Walter was my major customer. That year (1975) I had two colts for the NCHA Futurity. He owned them both. I had so much time on my hands that I taught Brand X tricks. I could make him buck and do all kinds of things. Thank goodness we wound up fourth in the Futurity."

The next year, 1976, Bill added a couple of reserve champion titles to his reputation. In the middle of that, he had the opportunity to haul Jay Freckles, owned by Jim and Mary Jo Milner, and the two ended the year with the NCHA World Reserve Championship title. He also trained a little mare, Doc's Becky, owned by Marion Flynt, and the pair split the NCHA Futurity Reserve Championship with Bill's brother-in-law, Terry Riddle, who was riding Freckles Playboy.

As Bill's business grew, the Missouri weather continuously hampered his training program, so in 1978, Bill brought his family back to Texas where he leased David Gage's barn in Wichita Falls.

"To maintain the consistency that I had started developing with the aged-event horses, I needed an indoor arena and Bob was reluctant to build one. I shopped around and made a deal with David Gage when his place came up for lease."

With every year, Bill's reputation as a top cutting horse trainer grew. In 1979, Bill grabbed his first NCHA Futurity Championship riding Docs Diablo, owned by Glenn McKinney. Although his training operation in Wichita Falls was well established, Bill did not feel that he had put down roots. He wanted to own his own training facility. Several years later, the magical performance of a dynamic little stallion, Smart Little Lena, provided the opportunity. Riding Smart Little Lena, Bill captured his second NCHA Futurity title.

At the NCHA Super Stakes the following year, Smart Little Lena continued his winning streak by claiming that championship. He then won the cutting horse Triple Crown when he and Bill tied for the championship of the NCHA Derby. They were co-champions with Peppymint Twist and Buster Welch, Bill's former teacher.

"Smart Little Lena gave me the financial security to make my own place possible. Daddy had moved to Era, Texas, and he called one day for me to come look at a place. Karen and I and Daddy and Gay (Shorty's wife) went to look at the ranch that is now my neighbor's. While touring it, I looked back toward Daddy's place and saw the house that is our present home. In jest, I said 'get me a price on that house and I'll buy it'. A week later the real estate lady called and here we are."

Bill and Karen and their three daughters, Tina, Erika, and Kimberly, moved to Rosston, Texas, where they live today. Bill continued to add championship pictures to his new office wall. In 1986 he once again claimed the NCHA Derby Championship riding Peppy Lena San and achieved co-reserve status on High Brow Hickory, a stallion owned by Hanes Chatham and Tommy Manion in that year's NCHA Futurity. In 1988, he once again returned to the Futurity championship circle riding Smart Little Senor, owned by Stewart Sewell and the following year, 1989, earned the Reserve Futurity Championship title riding Commandicate, owned by Ron Crist.

"Heart 109 planted the seed for me to return to cutting, but each and every one of the horses I have ridden prepared me for the next one. Every one I have been on, whether a great horse or a not so great one, has taught me something. That continues today, and I hope I don't ever quit learning about what works and what doesn't. I have been a fortunate person. I've had a lot of outstanding horses to ride as well as outstanding teachers."

Competing against 463 other entries, Bill captured his first NCHA Futurity in 1979 riding Docs Diablo by Doc's Prescription.

Introduction

BY BILL FREEMAN

I've never seen a perfect run, one with a score of 80. I've seen a penalty-free run many times, but since part of judging a run is the judge's opinion, I've never seen a perfect run.

Although the perfect run would be the ultimate high, my program isn't based on that goal. Rather it unfolds around the horse I am training, its physical and mental abilities, and its personality. Achieving the best that is in each particular horse at that particular moment is what makes cutting exciting. To have that adrenaline high of being able to develop and ride a great horse, to feel those gears work, and to have it all come together for one moment in front of roaring crowds after long hours of struggling, to me, is what cutting is all about.

To achieve this, you do the best job you can with the horse that is underneath you. Training a cutting horse is striving toward perfection, not having to reach that perfection. It's realizing the limitations of a horse, yet training him to be successful in spite of them. It's the thrill of feeling him take hold of what you are teaching him and the thrill of feeling the reverberation of the crowds in the coliseums.

Without the goal of the perfect run, there is no grand finale. Instead, each horse, each set of cattle and each show bring a new challenge, another opportunity to try to put together the ultimate cut and, while doing so, experience the thrills that cutting brings. That's what cutting is all about.

1

The Cutting Horse

The cutting horse is a unique animal. He is different in so many respects from horses in other fields of competition. To have that winning performer in cutting you need more than just athletic ability. Bob Loomis said this best in his book, *Reining, the Art of Performance in Horses*, when he stated, "There is a big difference in a horse that performs at a rider's command and one that works an object or another animal. The latter is a horse with more of a desire to work something. Cutting horses are a good example. When you ride a cutting horse and it does something wrong, you can correct it. But then you must turn it loose to do its job. That is vastly different than telling a reining horse, 'Do what I ask you to do and only that.'"

Loomis is a great horseman and understands the difference in the kinds of performance horses. To be a cutting horse, the horse has to have exceptional ability. He must also have a keen mind and plenty of heart. Take those three assets, train the horse to precision, add a lot of luck, and you just may win a cutting!

INTELLIGENCE

This sport is one of the few competition areas that requires a lot of thought process from the animal during both training and competition. In most arena competitions the horse is trained to follow the commands of the rider and his performance can be mainly mechanical. He is trained to listen to his rider and to perform on cue. For example, the barrel horse knows his pattern and runs around the barrels on cues from his rider. The reining horse also responds to the cues of his rider. The horse follows a predefined pattern based on the commands from his rider. Cutting, however, is not that straightforward.

Cutting involves a lot of thinking on the part of the horse. In training a cutting horse you cannot teach him a certain pattern that he will respond to time and time again in the show arena. During competition, his response is going to be to another animal, instead of to a pattern, and he must have a mind that can handle that response. He must go where the cow goes and he must be the one responsible for those decisions, not his rider. Although you can always assist and encourage, when that cow turns and looks at the cutting horse and the show begins, the cutting horse is on his own. Naturally, to get him to this point, you have taught the horse techniques and worked with his mind. But during competition, it is up to him to utilize those techniques and put that run together.

Trying to determine the amount of intelligence a horse has before he is in a training program takes some investigation on your part. Breeding is an important factor in this sport, and if the dam and the sire are smart horses, then you pretty well know that the colt is a smart horse. If you have been able to watch him play in the pasture, the way he reacts to everything from mud puddles to other colts will tell you about him.

If you are looking to buy a cutting horse, you usually have not had this opportunity. So after checking out his papers, the first thing I do is look at his eye. A good, big eye that has a soft look is usually a sign of intelligence, There are exceptions (I'll talk about those later), but 80 to 90 percent of the time, if you look at a horse that is winning, he will have a great, big, soft eye. It shows kindness and a willingness to perform.

With respect to minds, we often refer to "good-minded" and "bad-minded" horses. A horse has to want to use his mind constructively. If he chooses to do so, we refer to him as a good-minded horse. If he refuses to do so, we refer to him as bad-minded.

A good-minded horse is one that takes training well. When being corrected, he does not get mad at you and try to resist you. He thinks constantly and tries to make the moves that you want him to make. He wants to learn and he tries to help you by responding and learning during the training program. This does not mean that he is docile. Often, he may be aggressive, but he does not fight you.

A bad-minded horse is just the opposite. Although he may be extremely intelligent, you are going to have a fight on your hands. A bad-minded horse is like a person with a bad attitude. This horse is not going to take correction well. Even if you succeed in training him, most likely you will not succeed in getting him to use all of his ability in the show arena. He is smart and he knows how to work a cow; but he doesn't try to do his best all the time. After he has been to enough shows to learn the difference between the show arena and the home arena, he becomes "show smart." When you put your hand down to start your run at a show, the bad-minded horse is smart enough to know that you are not going to correct him there, so he puts no effort into the work and does not give you enough of his talent for a winning run.

(pages 22-23) A soft eye is often a sign of an intelligent horse.

(left) A good-minded horse wants to learn and please his rider.

21

A horse that has a lot of spark and try about him can take a run that would be marked a 72 by an average horse and because of his extra effort and hustle, he can make that run a 74. The bad-minded horse can do the same thing to a run on the negative side. He can take a run that would normally be scored a 72, and because he doesn't care, he'll cause it to be marked a 70.

DESIRE

Another trait of a good cutting horse is a big heart, having a lot of desire. Often this can compensate for a lack of physical and mental abilities. A horse with a big heart is a horse with a lot of "try." He will often try to do more than is physically possible for him just because he has the desire to perform. A horse with a big heart will go that extra mile for you. He's the horse that will not let you down when the going gets tough. He's got a lot of guts and he is going to give you everything he can in the show arena. He is the horse that is not going to give up when the cow is really bearing down on him, and he is not going to quit when he gets a little behind. His big heart will make him hustle just that much harder.

Smart Little Lena was a big-hearted horse. During a tough cutting, when he was really being tried, he was willing to give everything he had. You could always count on him to perform above the performance you'd expect from a normal horse.

Regardless of size, speed, or intelligence, a horse with a big heart gives 150 percent of himself if necessary. You won't know if a horse has a big heart until he produces it. No matter how good a horse is in the training pen, until you drop your hand at a cutting, you won't know how big a heart he has.

You can train around a horse that does not have all the physical ability that you would like him to have, but you cannot train around one that does not have heart. Without that desire, all of the mental and physical abilities in the world will not produce a winner.

ABILITY

Of course, you have got to have some physical ability to go along with the good mind and the big heart. The physical ability of a cutting horse has to do with his body and whether it is balanced. If the horse is balanced, he can make a good turn and pick up his front end properly. That is essential to a good cutting horse. A balanced horse is an athletic horse.

A horse with a balanced body usually has certain physical characteristics. His back is short, his underline is long, and his shoulder and hip angles match.

An example of a poorly balanced horse is one with a long back. A horse with a long back takes longer to turn around. Chances are, he'll turn around on his front end because there is too much distance between his front feet and back feet. Also, such horses usually don't have their four legs standing squarely underneath them. The legs are too far out in front or too far out behind the horse. This makes for

uncoordinated movement, certainly not athletic movement. To really be able to perform athletically, a horse should have a short back. It makes it easier for him to stop and turn.

Another example of an unbalanced horse would be one that doesn't have equal shoulder and hip angles. He might have steep shoulders, but good angulation to the hips and stifles. Such a horse would have plenty of power to drive off his hindquarters, but his front end would not have any reach. His straight shoulders wouldn't allow him to have any length in his stride. Therefore, the horse would constantly be pounding the ground with his front legs and not be able to use himself as athletically as a horse with a good slope to his shoulders.

The reverse creates different problems. A horse with a good slope to his shoulder, but almost no angulation to his hindquarters will have plenty of reach in his stride, but his rear end would not be strong enough to produce the power necessary for moving forward, stopping, and turning. Straight stifles and lack of hip muscling would hamper a horse in being able to stop hard and fast and hold the ground in his stops and turns.

A cutting horse's hocks are very important because that is where he gets his power to maneuver. He uses his hocks

(top) A balanced horse has a short back with matching shoulder and hip angles.

(above) A horse with a long back will take longer to turn around and do so with less power.

1a — A balanced horse with matching shoulder and hip angles can make good turns and pick up his front end properly.

1b — A horse with good hip/stifle angulation and steep shoulders has plently of power from his hindquarters but little length in his stride.

1c — A horse with a good shoulder slope but no angulation to his hindquarters will lack the power in his hindquaters necessary for top performance.

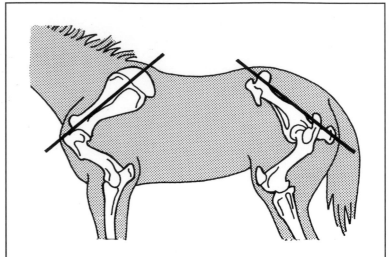

1a — Matching shoulder and hip angulation.

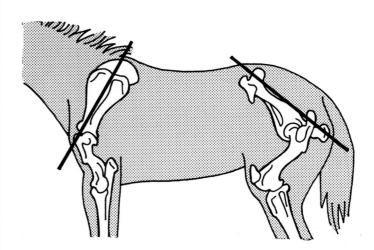

1b — Good hip/stifle angulation but steep shoulders.

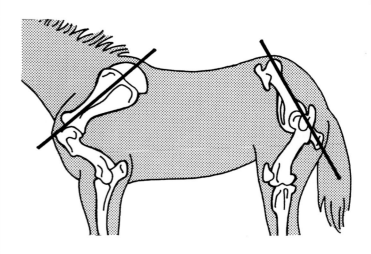

1c — Good shoulder slope but poor hindquarter angulation.

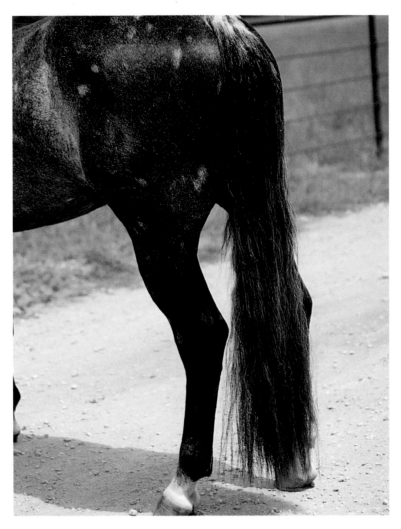

(left) Good hocks are crucial for a cutting horse. Strong, low to the ground hocks enable a horse to turn more easily with less chance of injury.

(above) A neck set too high on the shoulders can affect the balance of the horse while cutting.

constantly in the hard stops and quick turns necessary to control a cow. Consequently, there is a lot of torque and twisting of the hocks. The lower to the ground the hock is built, the easier it will be for the horse to turn around. The easier it is for him to turn around, the less torque there is. Strong, powerful hocks also help a horse to stop more easily. He can complete the stop without much exertion on his part. This means there is less opportunity for injury.

I like a good top-line in a cutting horse. I want a straight line from the horse's poll all the way past the hip. The way a horse's neck ties into his shoulder is important in cutting. The horse that has his neck tied into his shoulder too high will often carry his head too high. This is distracting while he is working and it will affect his balance.

The size of a horse's head can sometimes affect a horse's performance. A horse with a big head usually works with it up in the air, and that's a handicap in cutting. He won't be as limber and he won't look as attractive on a cow.

The size of the hip is not that important to me as long as there is some stability in the horse's hind leg. Of course, he needs to be standing underneath himself so that he is balanced.

Look at the correctness of the legs. You don't want to begin a venture with an extremely crooked-legged horse

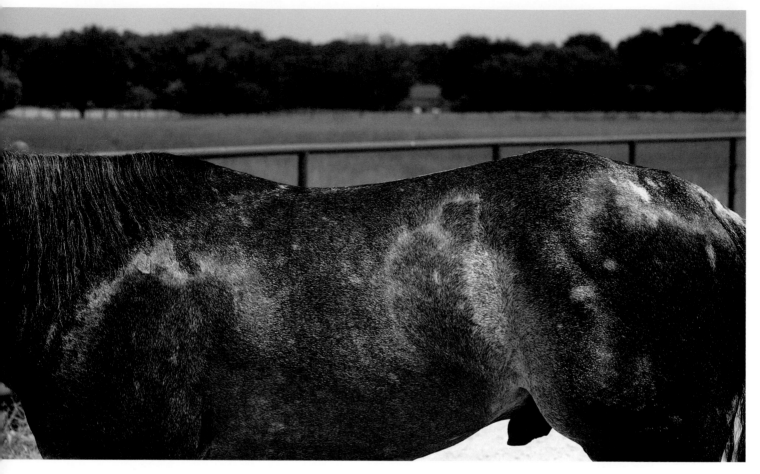

A straight line from the poll to the hip is referred to as a good top-line.

because you are going to have problems down the road. A crooked-legged horse will usually get sore often. If you continue to work one that is sore, you are not only damaging him physically, but you are also damaging him mentally. Even if he has a big heart, if you keep working him while he is sore, before long he is going to just give up.

I like a small horse, meaning one from 14 to 14-3 hands. A small horse is quicker and a little lower to the ground than a big horse. He can stop and turn around faster. He can do things and be finished long before a big horse. An agile and wiry little horse can make an error and recover from it in less time than the bigger horse. When the bigger horse makes a mistake, it will be exaggerated because of the length of his stride. With the little horse, it is just the opposite. His errors are not so glaring.

There are no absolute rules of thumb about proportion when selecting a cutting horse. Most cutters prefer to have a horse that is well balanced. But in the cutting arena, if you are working with an intelligent animal or one with a big heart, he will learn to compensate for his shortcomings.

There are exceptions to the above general rules about good cutting horses. You can't say that there are hard and fast rules that guarantee a good cutting horse. I've had some great cutting horses that weren't good to be around. Even a big, soft eye and a blue-blooded pedigree don't definitely spell success in the arena. Just because a horse has a big, soft eye does not always mean he is a good-minded horse.

It generally suggests that the horse has a good mind; but I've seen bad-minded horses with big, soft eyes, too. Usually though, those problem horses are man-made. They were not born with bad minds; they developed them through a bad association with man.

You can't just look at a horse and know it is going to be a good cutting horse. The registration papers can tell you whether other horses of similar bloodlines have been good cutting horses. I depend a lot on the horse's papers just to look for certain traits. I want a horse that is mentally trainable and, if other horses with the same bloodlines have proven to be trainable, then that tells me something. But that doesn't necessarily mean that the horse will be a pleasure to be around because, in this industry, some of the better horses have been real broncs. It just means that the horse has a better chance of being smart, and therefore, trainable. I follow my instincts when it comes to the way a horse looks. This is something every individual develops through experience and horsemanship.

It is seldom the case that you have everything you want in a horse. However, if I could have only two things, then I would prefer the good mind and heart. This horse will be easier to train and he will figure out how to win.

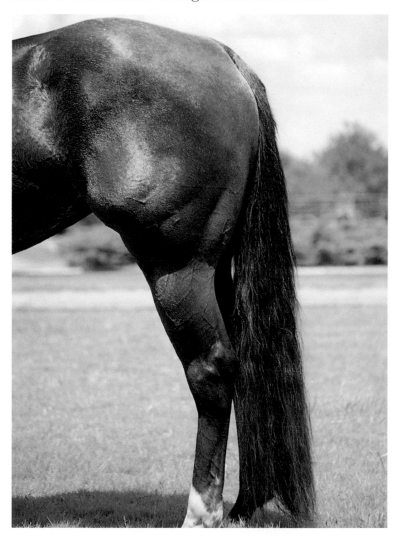

A good hip and straight legs help prevent injury as the program becomes more demanding.

2

Philosophy for a Successful Training Program

There are several things which can maximize the success of any training program. First, there has to be a lot of horsemanship on the part of the trainer. Second, because cutting involves working with the horse's mind and personality, the trainer must strive to understand his animal. Finally, maintaining a good working relationship between the trainer and the owner or non-pro is crucial.

HORSEMANSHIP

Horsemanship is the understanding of how a horse ticks. This understanding involves knowing how a horse thinks and how he reacts. A lot or people are born with a sixth sense about horses. We often refer to such people as having a "knack" with horses. They make excellent horse trainers, and often, good riding instructors. However, for those who aren't born with the gift of natural horsemanship, it's possible to learn a lot by studying horses themselves— their nature, anatomy, movement, etc. After a certain amount of time working with horses, you can develop instincts and intuitions about horses and see what works and what doesn't.

Good horsemanship requires timing and feel. Timing is the ability to perform at the exact second that something is needed. A good example of timing was the Fred Astaire and Ginger Rogers dance routine. Their timing was such that they didn't step on each other's feet. The movements flowed together as if they were one.

It is the same thing between horse and rider. You have to become a part of your horse because your movement during a run will encourage or discourage his movements. For example, if you push your body down in the saddle, saying "stop" to your horse, just a couple of seconds too

(above) Getting acquainted with your horse can pay huge dividends later in the program.

(previous pages) Allowing the horse time to think about his lessons is an important step in training a cutting horse.

early, your incorrect timing will throw your horse's timing off. Your timing, therefore, has interfered with the horse.

Likewise, during the training program, your ability to take hold of the horse or spur the horse at the exact second that correction is needed is good timing. That is when it is most advantageous to the horse. If your timing is off, you are likely to confuse him. If you are late with your timing, then you might interfere with the horse's next move. Mentally, he will have already gone on to the next move, so he won't know what you are trying to tell him. To a good horseman, good timing is second nature.

Although a lot of people are born with the uncanny ability for timing in horsemanship, I do believe that some of it can be developed through hands-on experience. Those who are not born with good timing can achieve it if they have a lot of desire. I believe this because even good horsemen, who have natural horsemanship ability, constantly work toward refining their timing.

Timing is linked with feel. In feel, there is a rhythm to things, and when there is a glitch in the rhythm, you feel it. A good horseman feels when a horse is not going to complete the turn even before he gets into the turn. If that rhythm is not there, then you know a problem is about to be created.

A good horseman who has feel can adjust a horse before an incorrect move takes place. He can sometimes correct a problem before it happens. In putting timing and feel together, you can say that feel is often more of a preventive technique, whereas timing would be a reaction to that feel.

Many good cutting horses are ruined when they are reprimanded for the wrong thing. This is often caused by riders not recognizing or feeling what the real problem is. I believe that before you do any reprimanding, you should stop and objectively try to figure out what is causing the problem. Doing this will be one of the most successful steps in your training program. Your ability to recognize and handle these problems is just as important as your ability to teach the horse to work the cow.

Reprimanding an animal without understanding the problem is the biggest mistake you can make. Often, the symptom that you see or feel can be deceiving. The first step is to stop assuming that you know what the problem is and, instead, approach it thoughtfully.

The two of you, horse and trainer, must have your minds on the same thought for a reprimand to be effective. An example of this is a horse that won't stop correctly, although he has been progressing nicely with his stops in the past. Let's say he is a stallion and he was noticing the mares in the pasture while you were loping him around before working him. You immediately assume that he is not paying attention to the training program and not stopping correctly because his attention is not with you.

However, before you reprimand him, you decide to give him one more chance. Since you know your horse very well, you pay attention to any signals that he might be giving you. As he once again starts working the cow, you notice that he is indeed paying attention to the cow rather than the mares. But now you are also aware that something about the way he feels underneath you is just a little bit choppier, nothing big enough to correct, just something that you feel almost instinctively rather than physically. Again, he does not perform his stop correctly, but you know it is not the mares in the pasture and his lack of attention which is causing the problem.

(top) If the rider's timing is off, he will confuse his horse and disrupt the horse's rhythm.

(above) When the rider's timing and body position are correct, the horse and rider are in rhythm.

31

A rider must know for sure what he is correcting. This rider has pulled the head too far to the left, elevating the head and causing the horse to move to the right. The rider is no longer teaching the horse, but rather confusing him.

You stop your training program and walk him around. Now that the other signals have alerted you to a problem, you become aware that with every few steps his walk has a certain hesitancy to it. With further examination, you find that the horse is beginning to show the first signs of lameness in his back right leg.

That entire scenario explains why you must know for sure what you are correcting and not just assume that you know. In this instance, the horse's mind was on protecting his leg from pain and your mind was on his incorrect stop. Trying to correct his stop would probably not have been successful since he was in pain. In fact, if you had pushed the issue, you might have further damaged the leg. The problem you saw, the incorrect stop, was a symptom of something other than what you thought at first. This is often the case in training a cutting horse.

Feel is also something that you shouldn't have to think about. In fact, if you do think about it, it's too late. Feel is related to the subconscious mind because it is a reaction rather than a thought. It helps to be born with feel, but it is something that a rider with lots of desire can develop.

Timing and feel are mostly learned through experience—trial and error. Your timing can be improved by repetitive work. Just like continually riding a horse will help you sit better in the saddle, continually cutting will help you improve your timing and feel for the sport.

Finally, a good horseman knows that on the back of an animal is not the place to display temper. Actually, a trainer who is a good horseman never shows his temper. The trainer who shows his temper is just demonstrating that he does not have the intelligence to out-think his horse. Therefore, to overcome the problem he is having with the horse, he uses brute force.

Anybody can do that, but it takes a horseman to back away from a problem, sit quietly, and try to figure it out. Maybe you need to change working places. Maybe the horse does not understand what the trainer wants him to do. If this is the case, the trainer needs to teach the horse the technique in another manner. Maybe the horse is telling the trainer that he is physically hurting somewhere.

It takes a horseman to hunt the solution rather than simply force his own method on the horse. It also takes a horseman to know that failure to find the answer to the problem the first time does not reflect badly on his training abilities. Rather, it enhances them since he is demonstrating his willingness to work through the problem instead of dictating the answer to the horse.

KNOWING YOUR HORSE

The mind of an animal cannot be dismissed. A good horseman realizes that he has got to get into the mind of a horse and know how he thinks. There are a lot of trainers who work without any regard to their horses' mental capabilities. They use intimidation techniques in their training. Such a trainer makes the horse work the cow according to the way the trainer thinks it should be done, rather than create a desire in the horse to work the cow using the horse's talents. Most trainers who operate by intimidation do so because they are not good horsemen.

A good horseman uses the mental faculties that a horse offers, rather than treating all horses as if they were the same. He acknowledges he is working with an intelligent animal and that his occupation requires deep thought in order to work with the horse's mind as well as physical ability. A good horseman needs a lot of flexibility to deal with different horse personalities.

You can learn much about the mental attributes of a horse just by watching him interact with other horses and with nature. Where one colt might balk at a mud puddle and not attempt to get on the other side of it, another will be intrigued and find a way around it. A third colt might not be bothered at all and just walk right through it. What you just learned about the minds of those three colts is that all three of them will respond to training differently.

owner/non-pro a realistic idea of what his horse is capable of doing. Also, it removes the pressure from the trainer to try to accomplish something that is not possible.

As a trainer, I try to offer several choices to the owner or non-pro when a horse is not progressing as I would like him to. I can continue to train the horse in hopes of improving him. I can suggest another trainer because sometimes a different program or approach might make the horse click. Or I can suggest starting with another horse.

To make a cutting training program work, there must be trust and confidence established between trainer and owner/non-pro—a trust that is just as strong when you are in the valleys as when you are on the mountain tops. If an owner/non-pro cannot put full faith in his trainer, if he continually questions the trainer's ability, it would probably be better for him, as well as for the trainer, to find someone else to train his horses.

On the other hand, an owner/non-pro who continually hops from one trainer to another will be doing a disservice to his horse. Every trainer trains a little differently and to continually subject a horse to different training programs will only confuse the animal. The owner/non-pro must develop enough trust in his trainer to give the horse and the training program plenty of time, since training for cutting is not an overnight process.

In picking a trainer, the owner/non-pro should consider his goals in the cutting horse business. If he wants to watch the training, he should pick a trainer in his area. If he

prefers certain training methods, then he must find a trainer who has similar training ideals. If he wants one-on-one attention, he should select a trainer with a limited number of horses so the trainer can give his horses more individual time.

The non-pro should trust his trainer about when he can ride his horse. This decision depends on the horse's age and the non-pro's skills. Often, it is better for the non-pro to have a horse to practice on, as well as his show horse.

Practicing on a show horse can create problems. The non-pro will probably want to practice more than the horse needs to be worked. Most non-pros need to work on their skills; but they need an inexpensive school horse for this.

Naturally, if the non-pro makes mistakes, his horse will make mistakes, too. This puts the trainer in the position of continually fixing the problems that the non-pro created. The trainer has to work the horse more, which tires the horse, and makes him not as willing to perform at the level required for a show horse.

All trainers work with non-pros differently, but in getting a horse ready for a show, I want my non-pro to work his horse so he will know what to expect. If he has been practicing all year on his school horse, he should be ready. Then I can teach him how to show his horse under the controlled conditions of the practice arena. The non-pro needs to feel the rhythm of his horse and learn how to get with him.

Matching the non-pro with the right horse is one of the best ways to help him enjoy the sport. If the non-pro doesn't ride regularly, he needs a steady, slow-moving horse and not the aggressive type a pro needs to win a major event. Although the slower type of horse doesn't have as much pizazz, he'll make fewer errors and, therefore, incur less penalty points. Such a horse will help a non-pro build confidence and develop his abilities. In time, the non-pro will feel he can handle the power and quickness of a higher level horse.

For me, a trainer's responsibility does not stop with the training of the non-pro's horse. I must train and encourage the non-pro as well. A trainer also needs to be a psychiatrist, a therapist, and mostly a friend to help the non-pro handle cutting mentally and emotionally. Chances are the trainer has experienced the same emotions and mental strain during his show career that the non-pro experiences.

Every facet of cutting affects every other facet. The attitudes and abilities of the trainer, the horse, and the non-pro all must mesh if the training program is to be successful. And the most unpredictable elements, the cows, will test them all: trainer, horse, and non-pro.

(opposite top) Good communication is a necessity between the non-pro and his trainer.

(opposite bottom) Non-pros and trainers visit the Freeman Ranch to work their horses under Bill's tutelage.

3

Control

Control is like an umbrella. It covers every part of your training program and your show performance. It begins when you walk into the horse's stall to get him and never ends until he is once again returned to that stall. Without this umbrella of control, your training program will be frustrating. It will also be difficult to effectively get through two and a half minutes of showing.

Total control of every situation in cutting must be in your hands. Your horse must understand that you are the one in the driver's seat, and although you want him to be an individual and take over the cutting, it must be within the parameters of your control.

First of all, control gives the horse security. If you are controlling the training situation and see that your horse is receiving too much pressure from a fast-moving cow which frustrates him, you can pick up the reins, slow him down, and gather him back underneath you. Doing this will give him security, as when a parent comforts a child who has had a scary but benign fall. Gathering up the child provides him with security. It is the same with your horse. When your horse knows that you are in control, you provide security for him just as the parent does for the child.

Second, control will make your horse respect you. He will be paying attention to what you are teaching him instead of allowing his mind to wander. We've all seen horses that did not respect their trainers. Such a horse walks all over you when you lead him, and he gets mad at every little correction you give him. The worse thing that can happen with a horse that has not learned respect is that he can hurt you. And just as important is the fact that a disrespectful horse is not in the right frame of mind to learn anything from you.

(previous pages) Bill corrects a shoulder-first turn by picking up the reins and bumping the bit for collection and control.

Using a little tightness with the reins helps to keep a horse secure.

When I refer to control, I do not mean that I make all of the decisions when my horse is working a cow. There is a difference between control and domination. Anybody can dominate a horse, but that is not what you want to achieve. When you choose to dominate the horse you pay the price of losing that horse's individuality, and you take away his will to think for himself.

When you control your horse, you direct him and help him to use his abilities more effectively. A trainer who dominates his horse wants to dictate every move the animal makes rather than to direct him. Dominating takes away a lot of desire from the horse.

You always want to maintain control while teaching each training technique. The technique helps you strengthen your control over your horse, since he is following your command.

For example, when you teach a horse to step across a cow, moving him in one direction and then returning him back to the correct position, the control is two-fold. With this technique, you teach him how to control a cow, while at the same time, he also learns that you are telling him what to do and that you expect him to do it. Thus, he is learning control from you.

Should he lose the cow while working this technique, I continue to guide him through the technique rather than allowing him to chase the cow. I have him complete the turn with a precise, complete stop. Then, I might encourage him to gather that cow back up. But the point is, I am the one

who makes that decision. If I don't show control in that situation, before long he will let his mind wander, not pay attention to the cow, and constantly get in trouble. By knowing that I am going to be there to encourage and help him in any situation, he is going to pay better attention to that cow. This will increase the crispness of his moves and his look of intensity on the cow.

It's like a kid in school. If he knows that the teacher is the leader of the classroom, then he is more likely to pay attention. If the teacher isn't the leader, then he might try to take over that role, and become the class bully so to speak. Then, too, if the teacher is a dictator, the student is not going to try to take over the role, but what he learns from the dictator will not be interesting, so his heart will not be in it.

It's the same way with horses. You have to find that middle of the road. Not enough control and the horse will not perform for you. Too much control and he will perform because he has to, but not because he wants to.

Control means breaking your horse to the cow. Everything in the training process relates back to the cow. Everything you do to that horse, in teaching or correcting, should have some reference back to the cow. You come right back to the cow after every move. If you take your horse off the cow, such as stepping him across the cow, make sure that you bring him back to the cow.

Teaching the horse this control in the practice pen can be advantageous later when you are showing. There will probably come a time in the show arena when you are going to have to help your horse a little. You may need to ride him harder to one side if he is getting short on that side or you may need to press him with your legs to accelerate. However, if you have control over him, if he respects you, and has learned the security of returning to the cow, any body signal that you need to send him will not make him wonder what you are doing.

Sometimes you can lose the control that you had with your horse. If a horse begins to "solo" on you, trying to do everything his way rather than listen to you, then you have got to stop his action and re-establish control.

(above left) After the horse has tried to solo, Bill reestablishes control by collecting the horse back underneath him.

(above right) After gathering the horse, Bill rocks him back and reestablishes cow contact by bringing the horse's nose to the cow.

41

Although the horse is reading the cow on his own, he still feels the security of the rider.

This is not to say that all soloing is bad. In fact, you are training him to read the cow on his own without waiting for a signal from you. However, soloing is bad if the horse is doing things his way rather than the right way. A good example would be not completing a stop. In a training situation, you always make the horse complete the entire training maneuver, even if he loses a cow in the process. If he did not complete the stop correctly, then you take control and have him do so. After the correction, then you step him back to the cow.

By correcting the sloppy stop, you have established in the horse's mind that you are controlling this training process. He will figure out that he is not going to be able to get away with sloppy stopping without being corrected. He will also soon learn that if he has to be stopped and corrected, he will most likely lose the cow and then have to run to get her. He will learn that doing it right the first time is just a whole lot easier.

As with kids, some horses may require a little more control than others. Since you are the trainer and you know what you want to accomplish with each horse, you must be open-minded, willing to experiment, and willing to make adjustments from horse to horse.

If you have a hot-blooded horse, you will really need to work with his mind to establish control. A hot-blooded horse usually wants to move too fast and overreact. Therefore, you may have to take hold of him by picking up the reins and bumping his nose or mouth to slow him down as he goes across the pen.

In trying to work the hot-blooded horse, you do not need to put a lot of pressure on him by moving him up into a cow. Instead, you need to help him relax as much as possible and slow everything down. One method to help him relax is to have him face the cow, but only after he has established a good stop. Then move him slowly up into that cow. Dry working (explained in Chapter Eight) will also help you to teach control to the hyper horse.

Everything ties in with control—getting the horse broke, teaching him about a cow, teaching him how to handle a cow. Control is not something that is taught once or used once. It's got to be established at the beginning and then enhanced and encouraged throughout the training program. Like I said, it is the umbrella over both training and showing.

Pinned ears and an intent expression show the determination in this horse to handle the cow. Establishing control throughout the training program develops this type of intensity.

4

Training Overview

My training program is geared toward producing a solid, competitive cutting horse, one that is capable of winning the NCHA major aged events. The program begins when the horse is an early 2-year-old and, although geared for the first aged event—the NCHA Futurity—I continue this program for horses that progress through the years to other NCHA aged events and week-end shows. You can take the techniques I describe in the following chapters and use them to develop your horse's skills, whether he is a novice at the sport or an old campaigner that needs a tune-up.

The first four weeks in my program include breaking the 2-year-old to saddle. This starts in the round breaking pen and ends in the pastures and on the trails with the young horse accepting a rider, learning where to put his feet, and following basic aids.

After the initial breaking period, I introduce the horse to a cow in a 60 x 60-foot square pen. He stays there until he acknowledges the cow's presence and shows some interest in moving with the cow. This usually takes from three to five days or as long as necessary for the individual horse.

From then on, I place the horse in a herd situation in a 120-foot round pen. The bulk of the horse's education takes place in this pen, unless he runs into problems or needs a change of pace. I use a 90 x 90-foot square pen to handle some specific problems and a 150-foot round pen for a definite challenge and change of scenery. That does the cattle and the horse some good.

Although I use several different sizes and types of pens, I want to emphasize that the pen is not the most crucial element in training a cutting horse. It's more important that the horse learn to work the cow wherever the cow happens to be. The size or shape of the pen is not vital. You can take

The horse learns to accept a rider on his back in the safety of the round breaking pen.

The 60 x 60-foot square pen is where the horse first encounters the cow. Since the pen is relatively small, it restricts the horse's movements and helps to focus his attention on the cow.

(previous pages) Bill teaches his horses to come back to a cow. Facing the cow, a horse tends to focus his mind on her.

any pen, round or square, and train a cutting horse from first breaking him to finally finishing him, as long as you make the cow the focal point.

If you have the opportunity to use several different pens, then use them to your advantage. However, if you don't, no matter where you train, concentrate on teaching your horse that his responsibility is the cow, no matter the shape or size of the pen.

With any of the techniques I talk about, progress depends largely upon the horse's mental and physical abilities and the skills of the trainer. Where one horse might understand what is being taught immediately, it might take another several training sessions to grasp the concept. There is no time limit to training a horse.

Also, I do not work on any one technique too long. If I grill the horse on one thing for a long time, he will get tired of doing it and possibly start resisting. I go on to other techniques, practice them, then return to any technique that gave the horse problems.

Many people think that to train a cutting horse you must work the horse as if he were in a show ring environment. That means you have the cattle behind you, the cow you are cutting in front of you, and you work parallel to the herd. I personally do not believe in this philosophy, and I do not train my horses under such conditions. Instead, I work whatever angle, or position is best to teach the horse to hold a cow. This means that I might work all the way around the pen, letting the horse and the cow I am working push the herd ahead of us as we go.

This overview of my training program is meant to give you a concise definition of my program's format. The details of the program unfold in the chapters. But you must understand that cutting is a difficult sport to explain on paper. It is mentally intense as well as physically demanding and everything happens at the same time. There is no pattern to follow as in most other equine sports. The element of the cow makes all the difference. So realize as you read the chapters on training that most of the techniques are introduced simultaneously. They interact with one another to produce the incredible moves of the cutting horse as he controls the cow you put before him.

Everything I do in training a horse to cut actually starts at the beginning of my program. By this I mean I have certain requirements that I want a horse to meet as we progress through the program. However, everything starts the first day that I introduce the horse to a cow. The program I start with is the program I end up with. In the beginning it is slow and seemingly unstructured, but in the end, it's fast and correct.

The cutting horse is taught to work a cow, not a pattern.

5

Breaking the Colt

There are many ways to break young horses to ride and this chapter is meant only to give you an overview of how breaking is done on the Freeman Ranch. I prefer to start training a cutting horse when he is a 2-year-old. When he comes to the ranch, I like a colt to be halter-broke, but nothing else. Like most trainers, I prefer to break the horse according to my program, rather than have him broke to ride by someone else. If someone else does the breaking, the colt might have learned habits that don't fit my training program. Then I must break those habits. This is not to say that the habits are necessarily bad, just that they do not fit my program.

GROOMING AND INTRODUCING THE SADDLE

I don't believe in wasting a lot of time with the colts in the early stages of the training program. My philosophy is that they have got to be ridden, so we might as well go ahead and ride them. Since this is a stressful period for the young horse, it seems to me that it is better to get it over as quickly as possible rather than to prolong it by driving the colt, or some other long, drawn-out method.

First, I halter the horse and tie him up, usually in a stall. Then, I rub him and handle him a little bit. I brush his back, legs, neck, hips—just get him used to having someone touch him. I continue with this process until I see that the horse relaxes a little bit. This may take five minutes or it may take 30 minutes, depending on the horse's temperament and how much handling he has already experienced.

It's good for owners to handle their young horses. It helps them get used to human contact and touch. However, there is a difference in handling a colt and spoiling him. A colt that has been handled properly knows about humans,

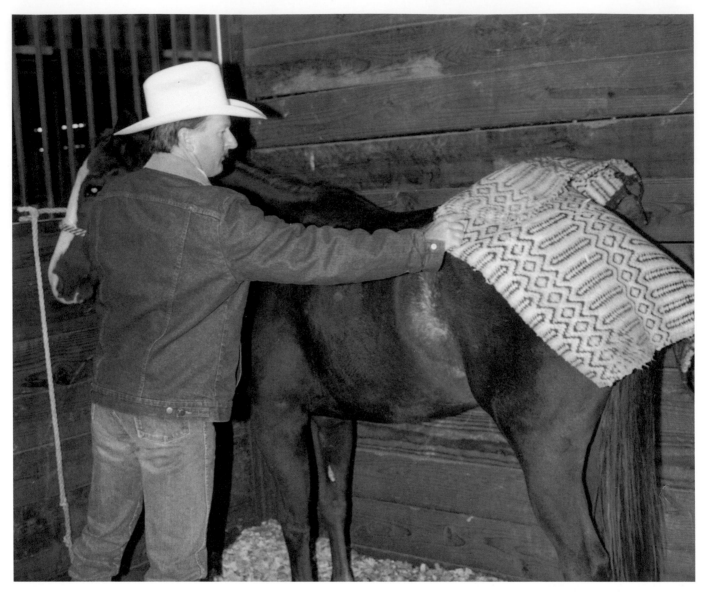

Sacking the colt accustoms him to having objects on his body.

(previous pages) Bill has kept some land on his ranch in its natural state. His training program includes riding young horses through the rugged, hilly terrain.

is not afraid of them, and respects them. He has been taught manners. He walks behind or beside his trainer quietly. If the trainer stops and stands still, the mannerly colt stands quietly, too, rather than acting restless or pawing. He pays attention to the trainer at all times, instead of watching other horses or other sights.

A spoiled horse is just the opposite. He has not learned to respect people. He has not been taught where to walk and, therefore, might try to walk in front of the trainer or even try to get loose. He becomes agitated when corrected and tries to fight the trainer, rather than respond to the correction. A spoiled horse usually has numerous bad habits, such as biting and kicking. He's undisciplined and might not stand still for saddling, spooks at everything, and in general, is a nuisance to handle. One wreck can lead to another. Such a horse is a danger, not only to himself, but to the people around him. His training program will be harder in the beginning since the trainer must re-educate him, correct his bad habits, and teach him respect.

As I rub and brush a colt, I don't expect him to be

completely relaxed, like an old gelding that has spent years around activity and people, but I am looking for a little change. I'd like to see his body relax, but this may or may not happen depending on the amount of handling the colt has had. Since this may be the first time he has ever experienced any touching and rubbing, he is still going to be fearful. But I do want to be able to touch him on his back, neck, legs, and hips without him jumping away from me. I want him to become familiar with having me on both sides. I continue rubbing and brushing until the colt is used to my presence. Gentle but firm touching and brushing let the colt know you are in control and will not hurt him. It takes time for some fearful colts to relax, so give them the time.

At this point, I bring a saddle and pad into the stall and place it on his back in a firm but easy manner. Some horses are more skittish than others about this first encounter with a saddle. Not being in a hurry, but being deliberate with your movements, helps reduce this skittishness. Be slow and quiet, yet firm. I adjust the cinch to fit snugly, so the saddle won't slip, but not so tight as to agitate the horse.

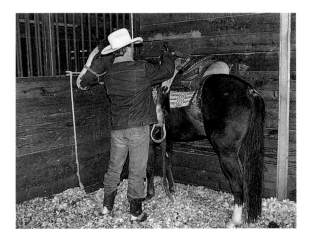

When first saddling a colt, Bill proceeds slowly but deliberately. This helps reduce the horse's fear of the new objects on his back.

THE BREAKING PEN

After the first saddling, I unsaddle the horse and take him to the breaking pen. The first pen that a colt sees in my training program is the breaking pen—a 45-foot diameter round pen with solid 6-foot high walls. Since the walls are high and the pen is solid, the rider is not as likely to get his leg or foot hung on a rail and get hurt while breaking the colt. I built the pen round so that there would be no corners into which the horse could run. Forty-five feet allows a horse plenty of room to move around, but does not let him really run with you.

I don't take the horse to the round pen saddled the first time because a lot of things could happen from the stall to the round pen. It might be best for him to not have a saddle on his back. Also, becoming used to me, the saddle, and being led to the round pen are too many new experiences for

The same slow, deliberate movements are used to mount the horse for the first time.

(top sequence) Bill first rides a horse with a halter and lead rope. He uses the lead rope to pull the horse's head around while introducing the horse to the pressure of his legs.

(above) The horse may buck the first time he is mounted.

a colt. He will be easy to spook at this time, and he might break away or even run over his handler. Therefore, I take the colt to the round pen with nothing but a halter on him. Once in the round pen, I repeat the saddling process.

FIRST RIDE

After the horse is saddled, I simply step up in the saddle and ride. As I explained earlier, this is a stressful time for the young horse, but it is something that has to be done. Therefore, the quicker we get through it, the quicker we can get into the training program for cutting.

I ride a young horse for the first time with only a halter and lead rope, not with a bridle and reins. I believe that the horse is making enough adjustments with a saddle and a rider on his back. I introduce the bridle and reins later. With this halter and lead rope set-up, I can pull the horse in one direction only, unless I flip the lead rope over his head and use it in the other direction. At this point, the lead rope really doesn't act like a rein or a training device, but is simply a security measure for the rider.

Most horses buck for just a little while during this first encounter in the round pen. A few of them, though, don't even do that. Each one has a different personality and some exhibit more fear and fight than others. This first mounting in the round pen may last 15 minutes or it may last 30 minutes. I am there to teach the horse to accept two new items on his back—a saddle and a rider. So I must stay with this plan until he allows me to ride him at a walk around the pen without bucking.

I also introduce him to the feel of pressure from my legs. After he has calmed down and accepted me on his back, I press his right side with my right leg. When he moves away from the pressure, I immediately stop pressing. I repeat this process several times while riding him around the pen. Then I apply pressure to his left side. Once again, when he moves away from the pressure, I stop pressing.

SECOND RIDE

If the first day of riding has been fairly successful, I introduce the bridle to the colt on the second day. The type of bridle is not really important. You can use a smooth snaffle, hackamore, noseband, or sidepull. What headgear you use is entirely arbitrary, since at this point you aren't

really going to control the horse with any of them. However, if his first day with a saddle and rider was extremely stressful for him, I ride him another day with the halter. Most of the colts, though, are introduced to the bridle on their second day.

On the second day, I repeat the same procedure. The horse is rubbed and handled, taken to the round pen, then saddled, and most likely bridled.

Now that I have the young horse accepting both saddle and rider on his back, I teach him to accept commands from the rider through the use of the bridle. I do this through repetition, since that is how horses learn. What I show a horse over and over is what he eventually accepts and what becomes habit.

Because horses learn through repetition, it is important that you are always aware of what you are teaching a horse. If you allow the horse to do something wrong rather than correcting it in the beginning, then you are teaching him a bad habit. An example is allowing a horse to move around instead of standing still and paying attention to your commands. If this is allowed to continue, then this action becomes a learned habit, even though it is a wrong action.

FLEXION AND THE AIDS

As I said before, most trainers like to break the young horses in their training program themselves. That way they can avoid bad habits in the first place. Not everyone breaks young horses the same way.

I like my horses to be flexible or limber in their bodies. Some trainers don't mind their colts being a little stiff. I do. When I get a colt from either the owner or another trainer who has already taught him that it's okay to be stiff, then I have to take the time to break the colt of that habit. How I do that is detailed below.

My main objective the first day with a bridle is to acquaint the horse with rein pressure on his nose or mouth. I definitely do not jerk on the colt. To teach a horse about pressure and to limber his body at the same time, I just use a gentle, firm pull. With my right hand, I pull the right rein firmly toward my right hip. I continue holding that position until the horse follows the pressure of the pull on his head. If the horse's body is stiff, I limber it by using pressure from my leg, just like I taught him on the first day of riding.

After I succeed in getting the horse to respond to rein pressure, I pause for a minute, let him relax, and think about what just happened. Then I repeat the lesson again and again until the horse responds comfortably.

After he follows rein pressure to the right, then I use my left hand and pull the left rein to my left hip. I hold it until the horse gives to the pressure and brings his head around to the left. Once again, should he need to be encouraged, I do so with pressure, this time from my left leg. Then, I pause and allow him time to grasp these new ideas. Allowing a horse time to think about what he has just learned is a major part of my training program all the way through. I believe it is as important as teaching him the fundamentals. After the pause, then I alternate the right pull simultaneously with the right leg (if needed), and the left pull simultaneously with the left leg (if needed) until I feel the horse following my commands with little hesitation. Naturally, I expect some resistance in the beginning, but with repetition, the horse will learn to turn his head in the direction of the pull.

To get the horse to slow down and stop, I apply pressure by holding both reins taut. The second the horse responds even slightly, I release the pressure. With time and much repetition, the horse understands my commands and learns to give to the pressure.

The way a colt learns to turn and stop, or do anything, is usually through a form of resistance. When I pick up on the reins to slow him down, he might do the opposite instead. He might go faster, especially in the first week or so of riding. When he does slow down, I release the pressure on the reins. If he gives to the pressure and gets an immediate release from his rider, he learns to turn and stop easily.

To get the 2-year-old to back up, I pull straight back on the reins. The instant he steps back, even once, I release the pressure. That might be enough for one day. The next day we can build on that one step backward.

I work to accomplish little goals. One step backward is a little goal. I wouldn't expect a 2-year-old to take several steps backward the first day. We have to work up to that slowly, one day at a time.

There is no set length of time that I do these exercises. I go to the training pen to accomplish a goal and stay there until I feel I have made some progress. If I didn't, the next day it would be twice as hard to accomplish anything with the horse. Eventually, I wouldn't be able to do a thing with him.

PASTURES AND TRAILS

When you start breaking a young horse, the first thing you have to overcome is fear. A horse reacts before he thinks. Horses run off and buck because they don't understand what's being done to them. When you're on a young horse's back for the first time, he sees and feels something moving on top of him that was never there before. Once you've conquered a horse's fear of a rider, he no longer tries to buck and he responds reasonably well to rein and leg

(above) Bill likes his horse to be flexible. Bending the horse's nose back towards his hip is a good limbering exercise.

(opposite) Another good limbering exercise. Bill walks the horse around in tight circles, pulling his nose towards his hip.

55

pressure, it's time to move on in the training program. This is usually done with one or sometimes two more visits to the breaking pen. When I feel I have enough control over him so he doesn't hurt himself or me, I move out of the pen and into the pastures.

However, at this time I just have a very green-broke horse, and since I do not have total control over him, I don't go alone. I provide the horse, as well as myself, some security by using a lead horse, ridden by one of my assistants. The two are not attached in any way, but I suppose you could pony the young horse off the lead horse.

The lead horse, a horse that is older, seasoned, and acquainted with the pastures and trails, leads the way on the first couple of outings. The lead horse is a baby sitter and we play follow-the-leader. When the young horse develops enough confidence in himself by taking direction from his rider and possibly even leading the way, the lead horse is no longer necessary.

Here on the ranch, I have kept some terrain in its natural state. The trails, as this area is called, are narrow, steep paths where the brush is often very thick. It's hilly, rugged, rocky ground. I take the young horse out there to help him learn the importance of knowing where each foot needs to go. He is ridden around trees, up and down gullies, across creeks, down steep grades, and between tight places. This is where he learns balance and how to pace himself. All I am doing is providing the opportunities for the colt to learn. This is a place where Mother Nature serves as the best teacher.

Out on the trails, I use the control techniques (turning right and left, stopping, and backing up) I started in the round pen. I use them every time we go over a tree limb, around a rock, or through some brush. In the pasture, the natural thing for a horse to do when he comes up to an object, like a tree, is to go around it. But he's never been taught when to do it and why to do it. With the help of the natural objects, I get my point across with the control techniques.

When you are doing all of this on the trails, you will probably get some resistance from the young horse. That's where the lead horse really comes in handy. The 2-year-old will naturally want to follow the lead horse. If the lead horse turns to the right, you use that to your advantage and pull on the right rein to turn the colt to the right also. Since the colt wants to follow the lead horse anyway, he quickly associates turning with the tug on the reins.

Backing up is also done on the trails. You can easily get into tricky spots in the woods and the only way to get out of them is to back up. A young horse usually can figure this out, too, and that makes it easy when I pull back on the reins to back the horse up.

Out on the trails, there are other things a young horse must learn to overcome, such as leaving horses that he has become friends with. The lead horse is there to act as a security blanket for the young horse, who has a tendency to be frightened and unmanageable on his first few outings.

I usually alternate between the trails and the pasture for about a four-week period. Riding in the pasture is fun for the colt because, for the first time, he experiences the freedom of loping in open field. Of course, this is quite the opposite to the challenge of the trails. Most horses that were really nervous in the breaking pen relax in the pasture and become quite mellow. Whether I am on the trails or in the pasture, I average about an hour a day on the young horse. The amount of time spent with the horse is a major factor in getting him broke. Between the trails and the pastures, he gets a lot of wet saddle pads for about a four-week period.

Riding through rough terrain quickly teaches the 2-year-olds to be attentive to where they step and to balance themselves as they climb in and out of gullies.

6

Introducing the Cow

After approximately four weeks of riding the young horse in the pasture and allowing him to learn balance and foot placement on the trails, I bring him back to the training pens.

60 x 60-FOOT SQUARE PEN

On returning to the training pens, you might say that I go from the lead horse on the trails to the lead cow in a 60 x 60-foot pen. This square pen is a little larger than the round breaking pen the horse first encountered. It needs to be larger because this is where I introduce the horse to a cow. The pen is small enough to offer some security to the young horse, who is learning about a cow for the first time, yet large enough to allow more room for the addition of an extra animal.

There is no herd of cattle in the pen, just one cow. This is the only pen where I will have only one cow at a time. I do this to allow the horse time to get used to being close to the cow, without becoming overwhelmed with an entire herd. Later, after he is accustomed to being with the one cow, the rest of the herd should not be intimidating.

The walls of the pen are solid, just like the breaking pen. The solid wall removes any distractions the young horse might have. It keeps him from being able to see other horses on the hot walker, those that are being warmed up, or those just grazing in the pasture. Further into the training program, and when he is a little more mature, I expect the horse to handle distractions without them interfering with his training. However, in this beginning stage, I believe the solid-wall training pen assists the young horse in keeping his mind on what we are doing.

Many people think that to train a cutting horse you must

When Bill introduces the horse to the cow, he uses only one cow rather than a herd. This is less intimidating to the horse. Once the horse takes an interest in the cow, Bill encourages him to go along with the cow.

work the horse as if he were in a show-ring environment. That means you have the cattle behind you, the cow you are cutting is in front of you, and you are working parallel to the herd. I personally do not believe in this philosophy, and I do not train my horses under such conditions. Instead, I work whatever angle or position is best to teach the horse to hold a cow. This means that I might work all the way around the pen, letting the horse and the cow I am working push the herd ahead of us as we go.

If you have the opportunity to use several different pens, then use them to your advantage. However, if you don't, no matter where you train, concentrate on teaching your horse that his responsibility is the cow, regardless of the shape or size of the pen.

DIRECT AND INDIRECT REIN

I teach a young horse to respond to my directions through the use of the reins. There are two ways of reining a horse: direct and indirect reining. With direct reining, you hold a rein in each hand, and guide the horse with direct pulls. In other words, to turn to the right, pull the right rein toward the right. To turn to the left, pull the left rein toward the left. This basic, plow-reining technique is always used in the early stages of training because it's much easier for young horses to understand what you want. Direct reining was first introduced to the horse in the breaking pen, so by this time he is familiar with it. It is further refined in the 60-foot square pen as the horse learns to work with a cow.

With indirect reining, also called neck-reining, the reins are held in one hand. You lay the indirect rein across the horse's neck and apply pressure. Tug lightly with the direct rein until the horse gets the idea that this is the cue to turn. To go to the right, you lay the left rein across the horse's neck as you move your rein hand to the right. To go left, you lay the right rein across the horse's neck as you move your rein hand to the left. The horse learns to move away from the pressure of the reins on his neck.

(previous pages) Gathering cattle should be done quietly and slowly. The cow's temperament will influence your ability to work him.

Circling a horse round and round, not spinning him, could also help in teaching a horse to neck rein. Also, the dry work (discussed in Chapter Eight) that you do with the horse and the actual cow work will teach the horse more about neck-reining than actually deciding one day to teach neck-reining. During warm-ups and actual cow work, the rein pressure becomes less and less and the horse will naturally pick up the indirect reining that is called neck-reining. This type of reining comes much later in the training process when the horse fully understands how to move away from pressure. I like to see my horses neck-reining by the beginning of their third year.

In cutting, the direct and indirect rein take on a specific meaning, whether you are riding with the reins in one hand or two. The rein that is closest to the cow, the one on the cow side, is the direct rein. This rein changes depending on which direction you are going. If you and the cow are traveling across the pen toward your right, the direct rein, the one closest to the cow, is the one that is in your left hand. The indirect rein would be in your right hand, the hand closest to the herd.

When you change direction and you and the cow go across the pen toward your left, then the direct rein, the rein closest to the cow, is in your right hand. In this scenario, the indirect rein would be in your left hand.

At this level of training, the direct rein is the rein I use in giving my horse direction. Just as I did in the breaking pen and then in the pasture, I teach the young horse to turn by using the direct rein to encourage him to come through the turn with his nose first. With a snaffle bit in his mouth or a noseband on his nose, this becomes easy. When the rein pulls the rings on the snaffle bit, the bit slides in the direction of the pull and the horse's head, with his nose first, moves in the direction of the pull. With the direct rein, it's easy to lead the horse across the cow—a technique explained more fully in "Stepping Across a Cow," which you'll find in Chapter Eight.

If you use the direct rein in training your horse to move or step across the cow, you will make things easier for him and also prevent problems from arising. But if you were to use the indirect rein (neck-rein), you pull the rein across the horse's neck. This encourages him to turn with his shoulder first, instead of with his head first. When he does this, he gets stiff, which causes him to sling himself through the turn. Naturally, this makes the turn difficult for the horse.

COW INTEREST

The main objective in the 60 x 60-foot square pen is to help the horse develop a desire to watch the cow. This is called "cow interest." Horses that are bred for cutting have a natural instinct to follow a cow. They are born with a curiosity toward cattle. But just as horses have different levels of intelligence and physical ability, they also have

The rein closest to the cow is the direct rein. Using direct rein makes learning new movements easier and prevents problems from arising.

Pulling the rein in the direction of the cow puts direct pressure between the horse's mouth and the rider's hand. The bit moves in the direction of the pull which causes the horse's head to follow.

different levels of natural cow sense. It's my job, as trainer, to create opportunities for a horse to develop as much cow sense as he can.

My goal is to have him watch the cow and move when the cow moves and I want him to do this on his own without encouragement from me. At what point the horse starts showing interest in the cow depends totally on the horse. Some horses pick up the idea immediately after several movements; others take more time and need more help from me in showing them what to do.

I can tell when a horse starts showing interest in the cow, because he'll start following the cow with his head. He'll look hard at the cow, expressing a curiosity in the thing that is in front of him. Perhaps, he is a little frightened of the cow. Whatever it is, curiosity or fear, he'll start watching a cow and following its movements with his head. Eventually, this translates to body movement with the cow. I encourage the horse with my hands and legs after he begins to move with the cow. The cow dictates the direction that the horse should take, and I direct the horse with my hands and, if

When the horse shows interest in the cow by following the cow's movements with his head, Bill encourages body movement from the horse with his hands and legs. His objective is to have the horse watch the cow and start to move when the cow moves without encouragement.

necessary, with my feet. In other words, if the cow turns to my left, I use the reins to rein the horse to the left and my right leg puts pressure on the horse's side to encourage his body to move to the left.

I keep this process up until the horse, on his own, acknowledges that the cow is there. The moment that this happens, I try to build interest in the direction the cow takes by having the horse follow the cow. I want the horse to react to the cow's movement and develop a curiosity about which way the cow is going to go.

Some horses are more adept at picking this up than others. Some are extremely slow and some are extremely fast. I would say that the average length of time it takes to develop cow interest is three or four days on cattle before a horse actually starts trying to react to a cow. It might take only one day for a horse to acknowledge that a cow is there, but three or four days to show actual cowiness.

But my goal is for the horse to initiate the move first without my help. It might be just one move. That might be all you get the entire work session. But I take it and build on that in the days to come. I do this by continuing to ride the horse to the cow. When the cow makes a move, I encourage the horse to follow. When the horse is rating wherever the cow goes, I have achieved my goal.

It is crucial to keep the horse interested in the cow during these early lessons. There is no set time limit to work with the horse, since each horse is different. One may really take to the training program, and I can work with this horse a little longer than I might work with another horse that tires more quickly or shows less interest. However, it is important to remember that all 2-year-old horses have limited attention spans. So you do not want to work a young horse too long and stress him. The average length of time in front of the cow is five or 10 minutes. As the horse matures, he may or may not need as much time to work a cow. Some may require more time, some may require working twice a day, some may require less time.

Although I might only spend five to 10 minutes with the horse in front of cattle, this is not the total time that I spend with the horse that day. Before he is introduced to the cow, he is loped on the warm up track just enough to relax him and work off any excess energy. This helps him to settle down so he is ready for business when he enters the arena. After I work with him, he is walked around until his body cools down and he is not breathing hard. This cool down period is just as important as his working and his warm-up periods.

MOVING WITH THE COW

In the 60 x 60-foot square pen, I never get the horse out of a walk. I put him in front of the cow, and when the cow moves, I press the horse with my legs and encourage him to move along with the cow. When the cow stops, I stop the horse, too. If the cow stands still long enough for me to work with my horse, I step the horse across the cow (explained in Chapter Eight).

If the cow runs off, I do not allow the horse to chase her. At this point I am not trying to teach the horse to hold a cow. During this phase of training, I merely introduce the horse to the cow and build his interest. Remember, in this pen and in these early stages, I keep the horse at a walk.

During this training process, I use direct-reining, with one hand on each rein. This provides a wide base of support with my hands which, in turn, provides stability for the 2-year-old. If the horse needs to turn right to follow a cow, I bring his head to the right by pulling the right rein toward my right hip. I encourage his body to follow his head, a technique he learned in the round pen. If he is flexible and does not resist the pull, then I assist him through the turn with my left leg. If he isn't flexible and resists the pull, I pressure him with my right leg to help him bend in that direction. This, in turn, helps make him more flexible. After that, I can use the left leg to encourage him to continue through the turn.

When the cow stops, or the horse stops the cow, I can direct the horse toward the cow, facing him up or stepping either at the cow's head, hip, or middle to create more movement from the cow. When the cow walks off, I press the horse with my leg or legs, using my hand to give direction, assuming the horse is showing cow interest. At all times I am trying to set up a situation to either stop the cow or cause her to reverse direction, creating an opportunity to stop the horse, reverse the "feel," and then go in the same direction as the cow. I am teaching the horse to stop, to turn and to control the cow.

At this stage in the horse's training, I don't believe the horse is capable of understanding what neck-reining is all about. I still use basic plow-reining to guide the horse.

In the small 60 x 60-foot pen, I've given the 2-year-old a lot to think about. I have done this using short training sessions to keep him interested, not frustrated. It is important that every day you continue to keep your program interesting for him, no matter what pen you are working in.

My colt will usually tell me when the 60 x 60-foot pen is no longer interesting. Things will start getting too close because the horse has learned to move more than the pen will allow him.

120-FOOT ROUND PEN

Following work in the 60 x 60-foot square pen, the horse graduates to a 120-foot round pen and to the 120 x 140-foot indoor arena. He remains there for the rest of the training program, with the exception of the times I use a 90 x 90-foot square pen or a 150-foot round pen to correct specific problems or for a change of pace.

Since the round pen has no corners, its main purpose is to give me the opportunity to teach the horse how to handle cattle. It also shows him that often what a cow does to him is in direct relation to his own movements.

I do most of my round pen work with the cattle against the wall. Wherever they want to stay is okay with me. I just work the size of the pen according to the quickness of the

(top) Pressing with the leg when the cow is stopped helps to bend the horse toward the cow.

(above) While moving with the cattle, the rider uses direct rein to keep the horse's attention on the cows.

cow I have cut. If it is a slow cow, then I can make the pen real small and create more pressure on my horse by working him close to the cow. If it is a quick-moving cow, the 120-foot round pen allows me room to back away from the cow. Since my horse is closer to the middle of the pen, this move is making the cow work harder than I am having to work.

In the round pens I introduce the colt to the art of tracking, and to the art of reading a cow. In the smaller 60-x 60-foot pen, the horse had begun to show interest in the cow's movements and had started moving with the cow on his own. In the 120-foot round pen I encourage this interest further. I am aggressive by nature and I want my horse to be aggressive also. I want to instill in him the desire to always think about the cow, what he can do to control her, where he can stop her, etc. I think you can make a horse a whole lot more cow smart by teaching him to be aggressive.

TRACKING

One of the few times that I use the 120-foot round pen as a round pen is when I teach the horse to track. I ride the horse into the herd and separate one cow from it. Usually, the cow will move toward the fence and then start traveling around the side of the pen. Should my horse not go with the cow immediately, I encourage him to do so by pressing him with my cow-side leg or in some cases both legs. Together, the three of us circle the pen numerous times. I teach the horse to track the cow by encouraging him to stay with the cow as we go around the arena. If the cow changes directions, I stop and change direction, giving the horse directions with my hands and motivating him with my legs if necessary. If I want the cow to change directions, I have my horse step out and challenge the cow, thereby making it turn.

Should the horse fall behind the cow, I press him with my cow-side leg to go faster. This is a press and release. If my cue was not strong enough, I press stronger next time, but always press and release. Should the horse get ahead, I take hold of him to steady him and gently slow him down. With time, and the length of time depends on the individual horse, my horse should pick up the art of tracking or staying with the cow, not getting ahead, not falling behind.

This is also a good time to teach the young horse about pressure and about pacing himself on a cow. After he is relaxed with tracking, I close the space between the horse and cow by moving the horse a little closer to the cow as we circle the pen. The horse soon learns that his close proximity usually causes the cow to react in a different manner. The cow may go faster, or try to stop, and go the other direction.

When I move my horse closer to the cow, he also realizes that the closer he is to the cow, the more steps he will have to make and the faster he will have to go since the circle he is making is wider. There are times when you need to help your horse accelerate to keep up with the cow or to step up and challenge it. To accelerate the horse, roll or press your spur with the cow-side leg. You can also get some bend in

(opposite) **Bill teaches the horse the art of tracking in the 120-foot round pen. This pen provides plenty of room for him to encourage the horse to stay with the cow as they circle the pen.**

his body this way. Rolling or pressing the spur is better than jabbing with the spur. When you jab, you shock the horse and cause pain. You might get some reaction other than acceleration. By pressing his sides with the spur, you won't take his attention away from the cow.

Moving the horse closer to the center of the pen and farther away from the cow, yet still tracking the cow, teaches him just the opposite of being close to the cow. He learns that he can track the cow at this distance and not exert as much physical energy nor feel as much intensity on the cow. Repetition of these moves soon teaches him about pressure and how to pace himself when tracking the cow. Obviously, the further away the cow is, the more relaxed you can keep your horse. At times you should step up into that cow and put cow pressure on the horse to see how he is going to react and to create more movement from your horse.

I will do this drill until the horse has taken hold of the cow, usually only three or four days. Yet, tracking is one of those basic steps that can be used throughout a horse's career. Later in the training program when the horse is experiencing too much pressure, or when you are trying to let the horse down or relax him, you can return to the basics of tracking a cow.

READING

At the same time the colt is learning to track the cow and pace himself, he is picking up instinctive habits of "reading" the cow. Reading is when a horse continually pays attention to a cow in an attempt to figure out what the cow is about to do. A horse that reads cattle is a mentally active horse. You can just see it in his eyes when he is cutting. A horse that is reading cattle won't have the look of the mechanical horse. A mechanical horse is one who moves when the rider asks him to. He does not look like he is thinking and acting on his own, but following the commands of the rider. Many times a mechanical horse will work the cow even if the cow isn't moving.

Much of a horse's ability to read a cow comes from his breeding to be a cow horse. Two things you can do to help him build this talent is to teach him to track the cow and to keep the program interesting.

(opposite top) When tracking a cow, the rider stays short, or inside, of the cow.

(opposite bottom) Move the horse into a trot or lope if necessary to continue tracking the cow. This is accomplished by a press-and-release action with the cow-side leg.

(below) A horse must be mentally alert to the cow's movement to "read" her next action.

7

Stops

Stopping is the most essential part of cutting. A horse must complete a stop before he initiates a turn. My dad told me a long time ago, "You have to ride a horse to a position to stop a cow, and once you have established that position, then you have to stop. The horse should take care of everything else in between."

Everything I try to do is aimed at stopping the cow. I don't think about trying to turn a cow. If I can get her stopped, I can control her. Therefore, in my program, a good stop from my horse is essential to a good run. A good stop means the horse has both hind feet planted firmly in the ground. He uses his powerful hindquarters to balance underneath himself. A good stopping horse is easier to ride, he can freeze a cow, and he makes the run look pretty.

If a horse is not stopping correctly, then he won't be able to maintain his balance and correctness. In addition, a horse that doesn't complete the stop usually circles or rolls toward a cow. Since he did not stop and turn correctly, he is now behind the cow and actually running her off or chasing her. In cutting I want to work with precise stops and precise moves, everything to perfection.

When you want to stop, sit down deep in the saddle, putting more weight in your stirrups with your heels down, your legs in a forward motion, and your toes turned out. At the same time, push your weight down in the saddle slightly and push on the saddle horn, never pull on it in the stop. Pulling on the horn will cause you to pull yourself up and become top heavy. Relax your upper body and open up your knees so you don't grip your horse. In other words, don't lock up your knees or clamp them on your horse's sides.

At the same time you sit deep in the saddle, gather your horse up. Prepare him to stop by gathering your lines with

some pressure. Then pull on his head while sitting down. It doesn't matter where the horse stops. As soon as he fully completes the stop, (parallel to the cow or at a 45° angle) move the horse back into the cow or face up to her. Remember it is the stop that gives a horse the power to push off with his hind legs.

I want to emphasize that to really achieve a good stop, the horse needs to feel your body. If you sit deep in the saddle and put extra weight in the stirrups, you can then make him stop harder and deeper because he feels you. I want my horse to feel my anticipation and be comfortable with it. This feeling is especially advantageous to the horse that is not a big stopper.

The most important thing to remember is to allow your horse to complete the stop before he turns with a cow. The cow, which is smaller, turns around quicker than the horse, but you compensate for this by using physics with your horse. The horse is larger and carries more weight so he has to use correctness to outwit the cow. Stopping and then turning places all of his power on his hind legs, which, in turn, gives him a surge of strength to use his stride to its fullest.

One of the reasons some horses don't stop well is that some riders think they don't have time to stop. To them, working a cutting horse is all done with continual speed and movement, but that is not true. In fact, uncontrolled speed and chasing a cow won't win anything, but it will create other problems.

During my training program, I want to build confidence in the horse to stop. I reassure him that it's time to stop by pulling on him with both reins and sitting down harder in the saddle. Then after he has initiated the turn, I try to accelerate him through it by using my cow-side leg for

(pages 70-71) Always complete a stop before turning with the cow. If the horse does not complete his stop, he usually circles or rolls toward the cow.

(top sequence) 1—The rider helps the horse to complete a good stop by collapsing his body into the saddle. 2—The horse is extending his front end through a turn which was initiated by the cow. 3—The rider caught the colt early in the turn with the right foot to change the angle of the horse to the cow. Notice both of the horse's eyes are on the cow. The horse is in a very challenging position. 4—The completion of the turn. The horse has balanced himself and started to catch a stop.

(opposite bottom) The horse has executed a good, balanced stop. His feet are planted firmly in the ground and he is using his hindquarters to balance himself.

By bumping the bit, Bill encourages the horse to turn his nose to the cow. Bumping the bit is not a technique designed to stop the cow, but rather encourages the horse to rate the cow and to be prepared to stop.

pressure, but only when needed.

When we reach the point to turn again, I repeat the same action. I again reaffirm the stop by pulling on him which makes him stay in the ground. I am saying to him, "this is what I want you to do, this is right. What you were doing is wrong." Then after he starts to make the turn, I encourage him through it by using leg pressure, but again, only when needed to adjust his angle or to speed him up.

These stops are often referred to as his ends. A horse that has been turned loose too long, one that has not been taken back to the practice pen for guidance and instruction, gets real shaky and loses crispness on his ends. That's why, when I am in the practice pen, I always help my horse. I like to reassure him of what I want him to do and by helping him, I am doing that. This usually involves the young horse, but also applies to the older horse.

Sometimes in a training situation, I bump a horse's bit with a tug on the reins when we are going across the pen. This is not to stop him at that moment, but to encourage him to think about stopping and rating the cow. If I really need to work on his stops, then I create situations in the practice pen that will give us opportunities to practice another stop. I do this by moving up into the cow and forcing the cow to go in one direction or another. As the horse turns to go with the cow, I can accelerate through that turn with my cow-side leg. Since I have moved the cow and at the same time hurried my horse, the cow will usually react and turn around after a few steps across the pen. Therefore, I will have created another spot to practice a stop.

The best assistance you can give your horse when showing him is for you to relax and keep thinking about the stop before the turn and continually watch your cow. Your timing will come from your cow, not necessarily your horse. You can initiate the stop with your own body and you are going to receive that information from the cow. When he starts to move, you move with him. When he starts to stop, you stop with him.

BIG STOPPERS

For a horse that is a big stopper, I cut a cow that is a little harder to handle, so he can move more and show off his talents. A slow-moving cow would not offer him the opportunity to run and stop, which is one of his assets. I do not want to change that which he does best. Such a horse may not really have any other qualities. He might not be real pretty when working a cow. He may not have charisma, but he can still be a winner.

I don't work hard stoppers fast in the practice pen. As hard as this type of horse stops, I would be taking a chance on crippling him or getting him sore. In his training program, I keep bumping his nose toward a cow, facing up as much as possible after completing the stops. I try to keep him real short on a cow, which means to work him on the inside of a cow rather than let him extend himself past the cow. If he has a tendency to get too flat, too parallel on the cow, he then has to extend himself all the time trying to make those 180° turns. By facing up to a cow and working him short, I am establishing more control.

I do this because I know that this type of horse is extremely athletic. I know that he can stop real hard so he does not need practice stopping. Therefore, I continue to work on his weak points by staying inside the cow and letting him learn to be smart about a cow. I want him to figure out what that cow is going to do all on his own. I keep shoving him into the cow, making him face the cow, which increases his intensity also. This horse is what we call the "blood and guts" type horse. He reacts rather than thinks or anticipates. I want him to anticipate a cow a little sooner than he does. That helps make him a more complete show horse.

To do this, I use all of the techniques I have discussed. I pull him across the cow (explained in the next chapter) using both my feet and my hands; I rock him back, and face him up to the cow, and I shorten down his turns through the use of angles.

This blood and guts type of horse will win his share. If the cattle are pretty tough, he is liable to win the cutting because he is strong and athletic. The "smoothies and pretties" (cutter jargon for horses that are flashy in their actions in front of a cow while they are in the middle of the pen) will beat him on a day-to-day basis because they do little things and make them look pretty. But they can't beat him when the going gets tough. His powerful stop will make him a winner in that situation.

8

Controlling the Cow

After you feel that your horse has developed cow interest and is moving with the cow on his own, it's time to refine maneuvers crucial to the sport of cutting. The following techniques teach the horse to challenge the cow and control the cow's movement. Remember that all of these techniques can be happening in the same time frame. I am simply breaking down each minute detail of cutting, which is basically turning right and left with the cow, and stopping the cow.

Figure 8

I introduce the horse to the concept of challenging and controlling the cow by using a figure 8 pattern. I usually start this from day one in the 60 x 60-foot square pen. The figure 8 helps initiate cow interest which we discussed in Chapter Six. As the horse progresses, this figure 8 will evolve into backing up and rocking back and stepping across the cow.

Hopefully, the cow will either be stopped or walking to participate in this maneuver. When the cow is standing still, I walk the horse toward the front of the cow, and then figure 8 by coming back around and turning back into the hip of the cow. Walking to the front will often cause the cow to turn. I can then follow the cow until he stops and repeat the process. If the cow doesn't turn, I have several options. I can walk straight to him and motivate him to turn and see how the horse reacts. Or, I can circle the horse right on around, bring him back up to the hip of the cow, and theoretically, I should be able to drive the cow. If the cow doesn't move, I circle the horse right back around and repeat the process. I am leading the horse with the direct rein in and out of the figure 8s.

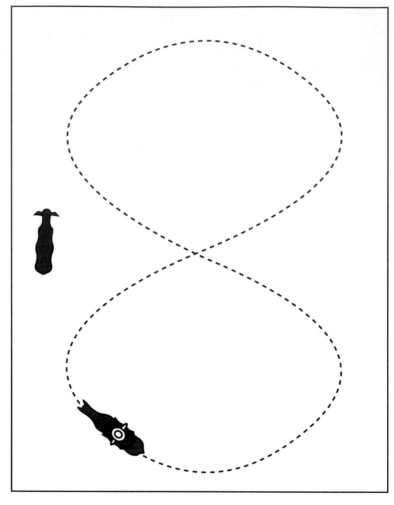

Bill uses a figure 8 exercise to introduce the horse to the idea of challenging and controlling the cow.

When the horse is responsive, willing to accept without resistance, I begin to tighten the figure 8 down. I go from a figure 8 to a bow tie. I make the figure 8 smaller and smaller until I have to stop. Then I start one step backwards and initiate a turn with the direct rein. I give direction with the rein first, then come with the cow-side leg. The cow side leg is used *after* you have nearly gone through the turn. This is how you can accelerate the horse on over to the left or right. Then I stop, back up, give direction to initiate the turn and if I need to motivate again, give cow side leg, but only *after* the turn has been initiated. Now, intead of leading the horse in the circle of the 8, I stop, back up and turn over...stop, back up, and turn over. It could be a few days or a few weeks before the horse gets the hang of this. Each horse progresses at a different pace.

BACKING UP AND ROCKING BACK

Backing a horse is not a subject that I dwell upon extensively in my training program, but it has its place. If you back a horse three or four strides before a turn, you can get too much concentrated weight on the hind legs. Then, when you release him for the turn, he has to elevate his body, almost like a leap, and he can get out of balance. I don't want my horses elevated or overbalanced so I back them very little.

(previous pages) A horse can perform crisp, pivotal turns when he utilizes his hind leg power by pushing with his hocks.

There are instances, however, when backing the horse quite a bit does become essential in the training program. For example, a horse might resist the bit, as we say, he gets "dull in the face." He lays on the bit with his mouth, resisting the directions or commands of his rider. To counteract this, I take hold of him with some authority, and back up until I feel that he has quit laying on the bit. I back the horse four, five, six steps, whatever it takes to get him to quit resisting the bit. I know that he is not resisting any longer when I get some "feel" in his mouth again. Feel means he is following the commands I am giving to him by way of the bridle, rather than ignoring me. The main thing is that you must get him to respect you, and in doing so, you may have to back him up quite a bit. This is one of those times when backing is solving a problem rather than creating one.

If he is really resisting the backing or just actually pushing on me and if I have a snaffle bit in his mouth, I may see-saw that back and forth from right hand to left hand to try and get a little feel in that face. If I have a bit on him, I may take the slack out of the reins to take hold of him and bump that face pretty hard three or four times until I get some reaction. If I have a hackamore, then again I take the slack up and pull left-right until I get a little feel on that nose.

When he quits resisting me, then I have his respect. However, a horse is a creature of habit and if he has done it to me once, chances are he will do it to me again. The repetition of this action is what will get his respect.

I like to rock a horse back for a turn, but I don't take three or four strides backing a horse through a turn. Rocking a horse back means to have the horse shift his weight to his hindquarters. I do this with a backward pull on both reins equally. He doesn't take a step back, but

(below left) If a horse is "dull in the face," backing him with authority until he no longer resists the bit should help alleviate the problem.

(below right) By rocking back—pulling backward on both reins equally to encourage the horse into a crouched position—the rider helps the horse gather his power underneath him.

rather gets in a crouched position on his hind legs. With both hands on the reins to provide good stability, I rock him back to almost squatting, then pull his nose around and extend him in the direction I want to go by giving direction with the reins. If motivation or acceleration is necessary, I press the horse in a left turn with my right leg after the turn is initiated. If I'm turning right, I press with my left leg again only after the turn is initiated.

STEPPING ACROSS THE COW

After the horse starts watching and following cows on his own, I start pulling the horse, or "stepping the horse across the cow." To do this, I choose a time when the cow is standing still. I begin by rocking the horse back on his hind legs. When he has shifted his weight backward, I start the horse's head initiating the turn. Then I can ride the body through the turn if necessary using the cow-side leg with a little pressure to be released immediately. This pressure is just to start the body on through. Then I complete the stop on the other side, 180° from where we originally started which would be parallel with the cow's hip. I am going to press him just a little bit to make him step through that turn a stride or two. That way he can get balanced again. Then I can get another stop, I can pull him back into the ground and go ahead with the same maneuver again—stepping back toward the cow or stepping up into the cow, rocking back, facing up and then continuing on with the cow. All of this is called "stepping the horse across the cow."

Then I reverse the process. I rock the horse back again by pulling on both bridle reins to get him to shift his weight. As before, I pull his head from the cow's hip across the body back to being parallel with the cow's head. With this maneuver he steps a stride or two out of each turn. If the cow moves, I do not chase him. I complete the maneuver if I am going in the opposite direction of where the cow is moving. After completing the maneuver, I stop the horse, re-engage the cow and then go with the cow. If I am starting the turn with the cow as the cow turns, then I do continue with the cow.

This is when the cutting horse training program really starts. This technique of stepping him across the cow is teaching him to move from his left to his right and vice versa. As we get farther into the training program, it will allow him to control the cow. What I am doing by stepping across the cow, is teaching control as well as if he steps toward the cow's hip, then the cow will move in a direction. If he steps to the head, then the cow should stop and change direction. In the middle of all of this maneuver, remember I am going to face back up to the cow at some time, whether it be at the head, the mid-section or the hip. Each one of these areas has a specific design for the horse to think about. If it is at the head, then we are actually turning the cow when we step up into it; if we step up into the mid-body, the cow can go right or left; if we step to the hip, the cow will most likely move forward. We are teaching the horse that his body positioning causes a typical reaction from the cow.

DRY WORK

Dry work is the process of taking the horse through training maneuvers without having him actually work a cow. This technique will help solve several training problems. In this situation, there is a cow in front of the horse, but it is not moving. I use that opportunity to dry work my horse or I might periodically work my horse when I am not in front of a cow, although I don't do much of this. I prefer to have a cow in front of me.

For example, I use a dry work situation to encourage my horse to think about the cow. With the cow standing still in front of us, I initiate my stepping across the cow to intensify the horse, to gain control of not only the horse but of the situation which, in turn, gives the horse more thought process on how to move a cow or how to stop the cow. The most important thing we are doing here in stepping across with the dry work is gaining control and teaching the horse how to move the cow and how to stop the cow. I do this two or three times, then I step him back up to the cow and let him work the cow again. The intent is not to increase the two or three times because then it just becomes monotonous for the horse or you can get into a fear factor, or the horse will just wait for you to tell him what to do. I want to step up to the cow after repeating this process two or three times to re-engage the cow and let my horse think "cow."

COMING THROUGH THE TURN

As you continue to teach your horse to turn right and turn left, which you introduced when you were stepping him across the cow, it is essential that he learn how to come through the turn correctly. I teach a horse to turn correctly by bringing his nose around first. Another way to say this is "coming through the turn with his nose first." I want his nose to be the first thing that starts making the turn. The remainder of the horse's body should follow.

I actually start teaching this maneuver when I teach a horse to step across a cow. If I want the horse to turn right, then I use the right rein and pull the nose in that direction while using my left leg to encourage the rest of his body through the turn. I press with the leg and then release. Never keep your leg on a horse for any length of time.

If a horse does not come through a turn with his nose first, then he is probably coming though the turn with his shoulder first. This is a bad habit and creates problems. Coming with the shoulder first is more difficult for the horse than coming with his nose first. It requires him to exert more energy, by kind of slinging himself through the turn. And, it is a stiffer movement; it does not have the flexibility and the smoothness that a horse turning with his nose first has.

CLEAN-MOVING FRONT END

When talking about a horse's front end, I am referring to the front part of the horse—his front legs, chest, shoulders, head. Moving his front end refers to the horse's method of turning. A proper turn is accomplished with the hindquarters remaining stationary as the front end pivots

A cow that is standing still offers an excellent opportunity to teach your horse with dry work. When you dry work a horse, you take the horse through some maneuvers correctly without corresponding the maneuver to the movement of the cow. Dry working allows the rider to gain control and teach the horse how to stop and move the cow.

(above) **Pulling the right rein tips the horse's nose back to the cow.**

(top right) **The horse begins a turn correctly, leading with his nose first.**

(bottom right) **Another example of a correct turn where the horse leads with his nose first.**

around them. To perform this pivotal turn, the horse pushes off his hind legs, since that is where the horse's power comes from. When the cow turns in the opposite direction, the horse turns too, by picking up his front end from the parallel or semi-parallel position that he previously had with the cow and turning cleanly. He can make as small a turn as 20° or as large as 180°. It does not matter what radius the turn is as long as the horse picks up his front end and moves it cleanly. This move puts the horse back in front of the cow again in a parallel or semi-parallel position.

When a horse moves his front end cleanly in a turn, he moves with a flowing motion, a motion that is not binding, scrambling, or choppy in appearance. I teach him to move his front end in a clean manner by moving him from one side to the other in one full motion. I don't want him touching the ground in between pushing off from one side and landing on the other. I stop the horse, rock him back, use a direct rein to pull his nose around. The indirect rein will be holding steady and rocking back until the turn is initiated and then it will be released. I accelerate him with my cow-side leg only if necessary. Then I am prepared for another stop, and I repeat the process.

In this movement, I do not allow the horse to make several choppy steps or to scramble when I am moving him across a cow. Instead, I encourage him to go from his right side to his left side in one movement, then from his left side to his right side in one movement. A horse that has a clean-moving front end is stepping across the cow in one fluid movement, rather than several choppy movements.

(above) By folding her legs up underneath herself, this horse maintains a clean-moving front end.

(below) A horse should move from side to side in one flowing motion without scrambling.

(right) The horse is moving in a collected, well-balanced manner. He steps across the cow in one fluid movement, rather than several choppy movements.

(far right) The horse's movement is completely unbalanced. He has shifted most of his body weight to his front end.

A clean-moving front end is necessary for a graceful, balanced move. A horse does not have to be extremely athletic to have a clean-moving front end, but he does have to be balanced. Practice ultimately results in the flowing motion you want to achieve.

I stress this technique from the beginning because it makes it so much easier for the horse to work a cow, and that helps the horse to have confidence. Even a hot-blooded or radical-moving horse will be able to handle cattle easier if he has a clean-moving front end. Later, when the horse is working under show conditions, moving his front end in a balanced, clean manner will give his run a more polished look.

Besides making it easier for your horse to handle cattle, a clean-moving front end closes the door for other mistakes. A horse that is choppy in moving his front end is one that has shifted most of his body weight on his front end. Other commonly used terms for this are "down on the front end" or "heavy on the front end." A horse that moves like that creates problems for himself. The choppiness will cause him to get behind a cow, be late turning with a cow and eventually get beat. Nor does it look good.

To get a better idea of what the horse is contending with when he gets down on his front end, try an experiment. Run a few steps with your body upright and your weight balanced as you normally would and stop quickly. Now run the same steps again, only this time, throw your upper torso out in front of your feet and try to stop quickly. You will feel off-balanced and have trouble stopping. The same principle applies to your horse when he moves his front end.

When a horse is getting down on his front end, it is almost like he is thrusting forward toward the cow. This action will scare the cow and cause it to run. Instead of trapping the cow in the middle of the pen and working it, your horse will have to chase the cow from side to side. With every turn the horse makes and every fall on his front end, he will re-emphasize the thrusting effect and reinforce the fear in the cow and her desire to run. Needless to say, this is exactly opposite the working situation that you are trying to create. Therefore, not only will a clean-moving front end help your horse move easier and look better, it will also stop many problems before they ever get started.

FACING UP TO A COW

The object of working a young horse is to teach him about the cow. To do this, you must put him in the position that makes him think about and react to the cow as much as possible. I call that "facing up to a cow." The chances are better that the horse is thinking about the cow when he is facing it than when he is turned to the side or parallel. Although a horse has vision that allows him to see almost 180°, that ability does not guarantee that he has the cow on his mind. Therefore, I want my horse to come back to facing the cow after every move he makes.

After the horse has turned to stop the cow and the cow has responded and completely stopped, many trainers want their horses to remain in a parallel position with the cow. I don't. Instead, after my horse has stopped the cow, I want him to turn his body back so that he is at a 90° angle with the cow; he is facing up to her.

Anytime a rider can get the horse to face up on his own, it cuts the horse's turn time. Facing a cow becomes a safe zone for the horse.

In my opinion, this is the only safe position to be in. I want to have control of the horse so that I can step him off to the right or off to the left should I need to do so, and I cannot do that unless he is facing the cow. The way that I do this after he is faced up is to ask him to step into that cow, thereby creating a move and direction which I can then override. I do not mechanically ride a horse left or right whenever I want to. Everything is improvised off the move or the direction that the cow gives me. I want him to think that facing the cow is his safe zone; so when he completes a turn, he automatically wants to move back to the position of facing up to a cow.

There are numerous advantages to having my horse return to the safety zone. Should the cow fail to move, I can now ride the horse straight to the cow. Not only will this probably make the cow move, but it will also put pressure on my horse, which will make him look more intense. By having my horse face up to the cow, both of the horse's eyes and ears will be on the cow. Every time I step toward the cow, my horse should feel pressure since he has learned that stepping toward the cow will most likely make the cow move. As he matures in his training program, the anticipation of impending action will cause his body to start lowering to the ground in a crouching position. He is getting ready to spring into action. This looks great in the show pen.

In working with any horse, I try to have him do what he does best. Accentuate the positive, so to speak. There are horses that aren't great going across the pen, but are impressive when they stay in the middle of the cow. I want such a horse to think about only one move at a time. I want him to try to keep the cow under control so he doesn't have to go across the pen. Facing up to a cow helps do this. Every time we get a cow stopped, I want him to come right back to her and face up. I start to move him back to facing the cow as soon as I get my stop. I let him read and think about the cow for a second and then move him to the cow's hip and step into, or toward, that hip. This should make the cow move in the opposite direction. In doing that, I am telling my horse where the cow is going so that he can get ready for the move. Facing up to the cow should hopefully make him a smarter horse.

Facing up to a cow leads to stepping into a cow. This is simply the act of moving your horse toward the cow. Stepping into a cow gives your horse the opportunity to control the cow as best he can. It also assures me that he has his mind on the cow and is concentrating on it. I want to be in control of my own destiny and having my horse take the first step allows me to do this.

You should only step into a cow when the horse has come to a complete stop. You don't want a fast, jumpy move with this step because that will have a tendency to make the cow run. Instead, encourage your horse to take a firm, quiet, hesitant step. This will accomplish two things. First, the cow will make some kind of movement, which was your objective. Second, if the horse is exhibiting caution and smoothness with his step, he will draw the cow to him.

Facing up to a cow and stepping into a cow are just two of the techniques in the program of teaching the horse to turn right, turn left, and stop. You progress with these maneuvers through the colt's 3-year-old year.

DRAWING

I try to encourage the act of "drawing." Drawing is one of those natural abilities that every trainer hopes his cutting horses have. It is kind of a mesmerizing effect that a horse can have on a cow by the horse's natural reluctance to step toward the cow. This cautious air presented by the horse causes the curious cow to move closer to the horse, thus being "drawn" to him.

A horse that works quietly and smoothly will make a cow curious and draw the cow toward him without scaring the cow. Working in a small area helps to instill this natural ability of draw in the horse. This happens because the horse learns that if he moves toward the cow, the cow is going to move away. He also learns that when the cow moves, his rider will make him move also. Therefore, in anticipation of what the cow might do, he moves cautiously and reluctantly toward the cow, developing draw in these movements. A horse that develops the ability to really draw a cow will have a lot of command and presence in front of a cow.

The ability of a horse, when you actually step him into a cow, to squat and get lower to the ground is that mesmerizing action that you are really after. Intensity is created by drawing. Another way to encourage this from the round pen is by stepping into that cow three or four strides until you feel that horse just step up and relax and start travelling toward that cow. Then you can gather him, back him off of that cow two or three steps, step him across that cow left-right and just keep repeating this process. Step him up to the cow, back him away, step to your left, to your right, back him off, face him up, step back to the cow. Eventually, this horse will get very, very hesistant in stepping up to the cow.

INTENSITY

As you progress further into the training program, your horse will mature with time and training, and he will develop intensity as he works. Intensity is the degree of concentration you try to maintain in the horse with respect to the cow. You do this by having the cow put pressure on him or you put pressure on him. This is not done through fear, but through respect and understanding of what a cow can do. In training a horse, you are trying to create the concentration and intensity to control a cow. By driving the horse to the cow, by keeping his feet to the fire, by trying to make him anticipate the cow, you are creating intensity.

You can't continually keep this pressure on your horse. There are times when you should allow your horse to relax. Slow down and release the pressure from him. Your training program must be a situation where you give and you take. You want him to have fun cutting the cow. But in the show ring or when you're preparing him just before a show, then you want to return to these techniques to increase the

intensity in him so he can be a winner.

You can visually see the intensity in a horse. As you start to move the horse up to the cow and the horse starts to anticipate the cow's movements, his body position will lower toward the ground. Stepping into the cow definitely creates intensity. If you are not getting the intensity you want out of your horse, then he may not be "hooked up" to the cow. Hooked up means the horse's full concentration and focus are on the cow. If your horse is not hooked, do a little dry work. Using your left hand, pull the horse's nose to the left and coordinate that movement with pressure from your right foot on the horse's side. Then reverse the process to the right. With the right hand, pull the horse's nose to the right and coordinate the left foot with that movement. Do this several times aggressively and then step him up to the cow again, letting him know it's time to go to work. You can also press your foot in the horse's shoulder to move his front end and cause him to become more intense.

One way that I increase the intensity of my young horses is to change from the snaffle bit after they have learned most of the basic techniques. I do this during the spring of their 3-year-old year, about March or April. I put all of my horses into a Clapper bit for a few days. (See chapter on Tack and Equipment) The change to this bit usually advances the horse by 30 days over what it would take with the snaffle or side pull.

The reasoning for this is that cutting is really a mental, not a physical, game. Using the Clapper bit, you can make the horse grow up tremendously in his attitude and thinking in just one application. That is not to say he will be that way tomorrow when you change back to the snaffle, but he grows up fast with the Clapper bit. The bit is heavier than a snaffle bit and, therefore, demands more of an instant response on the part of the horse. This instant respect creates an attitude adjustment for the horse and makes him work more like an older horse would.

As trainers, we have a tendency to protect our horses, but at some point you have to advance them. If you inject a little bit of advancement at different times throughout the year, you will be helping them to mature and commanding their respect at the same time.

(opposite) The intensity is visible in the head-to-head action between this horse and cow. The horse's lowered body position and concentration show that he is hooked to the cow.

9

Working Angles

For me, it really doesn't matter what kind of pen—square, round, egg shape, or pasture—I am still going to do the same thing. Where the fence happens to be is of no consequence. I just work the cow in front of me. The training technique that allows me to do this is what I call "working angles."

I work a lot of angles which allows me to trap, or control, a cow wherever I go and I am constantly thinking about that. I use angles to change the direction of my horse while working the cow. Rather than continually working parallel to the cow, I will angle my horse to allow him a better chance to head the cow and thus set up a working situation.

I do this by using a little cow-side leg pressure in the turn to step the horse up into the cow and challenge the cow. The cow-side leg pressure in the turn restricts the horse's turn radius. There will be more motion up and toward the cow and less across and away from the cow. I have effectively shortened the turn. Also, it changes the angle of my working position. The horse then, does not have a tendency to over-rotate, or turn too far, and thereby lose his ability to challenge the cow. How quickly you use that leg in the turn will depend on where you want to wind up.

For example, say the horse stops and initiates a right hand turn. As soon as the turn is initiated, if you press with the left leg, it will put you into a very challenging position up into that cow, probably at approximately 100° to 110° at the completion of the turn.

I prefer to use leg pressure when a horse is at a 45° to 90° angle to the cow. That is the "sweet spot." Using your leg at 45° from the start of the turn will kick the horse around to 125° to 130° on the other side. The area between the two provides a really good working position.

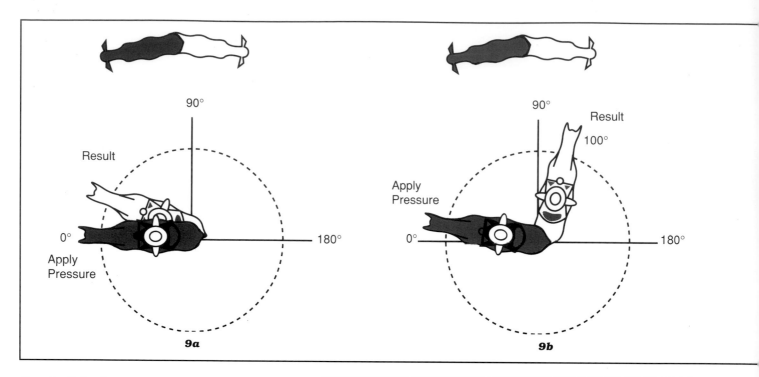

9a

9b

9a—Applying leg pressure too soon or before the turn is initiated could cause the horse to quit or roll into the cow.

9b,c,d—After the turn has started, you may use the cow-side foot at any time. The result will be seen approximately 90° from the point of pressure.

(right sequence) After the turn is initiated, the rider will use his left leg to change the angle up into the cow as shown at bottom.

(previous pages) Although application of the leg will accelerate the horse, it can also be used to intensify and change the angle.

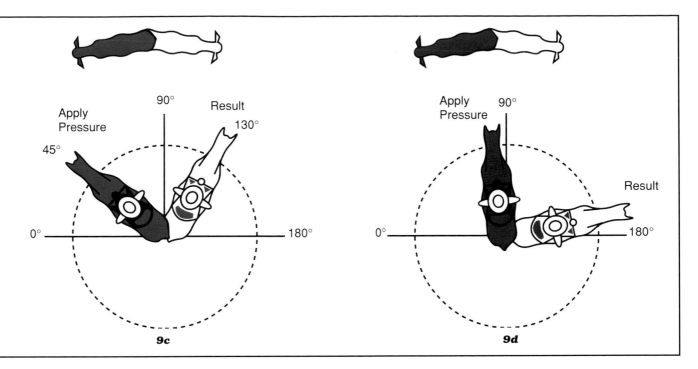

9c

9d

If you want to rotate the horse on around into a more parallel position, then you would wait longer to use that cow-side leg, almost into a 90° situation before you would initiate the leg action. This pushes the horse on through the turn to 180° from point 0° on the left hand side of the cow. You could even over-rotate the horse with the leg at this point and get more extension.

When using leg pressure, you must release the pressure quickly or this will also cause you to overdo the rotation. A horse has the natural ability to turn around just so far. How you set that horse up on the cow will determine how far around that angle is going to come. You can ask him to turn too far from one side to another. For example, if he is too flat on one side and you ask him to turn 180° or more, then he is going to scramble, using choppy little steps. Continually shortening that angle helps him not to have to make big 180° turns. This puts you ahead of the ball game.

It is seldom that a horse needs to make that big 180° turn. You might desire a larger turn to angle the horse farther away from a cow in order to reduce the pressure that you are putting on the cow, or to reduce the pressure that the horse is feeling from the cow. Then, after the pressure is off and I see the cow relaxing or feel my horse relaxing a bit, I can ease my horse over by the use of angles and find a spot where I can trap the cow again and increase the intensity once more.

It is a matter of slowing down to be able to speed up. Since you rarely have that perfect cow, you have to continually feel and find where you can get hold of the cow you have and make her work for you. You will often have one that is wandering around the pen and paying little attention to your horse, or you will have one that is trying you. It is a matter of giving and taking, a matter of accelerating and slowing down. You give a little pressure to the cow; you

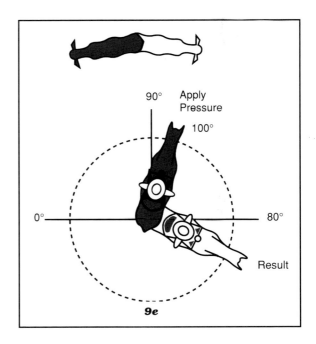

9e

9e—Occasionally you might need to over-rotate the horse to get more extension.

remove the pressure; you work close to the cow to accelerate the action; you back away from the cow to slow down the action. These are ways of finding where you can get control of the cow. This applies both in training and showing.

After the early basics of tracking, pacing, and reading a cow have been accomplished, I begin working the 120-foot round pen just like a square pen most of the time, because I am constantly working angles. Working angles just means changing the working position of your horse as you need to, whether it is to create training opportunities or to reduce pressure. Although working angles requires me to direct the horse at the proper time, the horse has previously learned how to manuever correctly so that he can follow my command. He learned this when I taught him to step across a cow and to move his front end correctly and cleanly.

In my training program, whether it is by my movements or the horse's movements, it is a matter of teaching a horse to work a cow rather than teaching a horse to work a pattern. The main point to remember is that the shape of the pen you use is not as important as the kind of technique you use in training a cutting horse. It is the method and not the place that teaches.

By changing angles, I can make the pen bigger or smaller. This is important later when you are under show conditions. I can get control in the show pen because the horse is used to me changing angles on him in the working pen. If there is too much cow pressure on my horse, then I back away and slow down, giving my horse more time to think. Putting more distance between my horse and the cow slows things down and removes pressure. This in itself is a method of changing angles. Using this technique, I am playing defense.

(opposite) **The horse has checked the cow and is in a great position to either stop the cow, or if the cow doesn't stop and turn, to continue onto a parallel position.**

(below) **The horse has established a good angle to work the cow.**

10

Over-Rotation

A horse over-rotates when he makes the mistake of turning too far. Visualize a circle, which is a total of 360°. Half of that circle is 180°. This is the imaginary plane across the pen—an invisible straight line on which you work your horse. Any time a horse rotates, or turns, more than the 180° while working a cow, he has over-rotated.

This 180° area is the maximum area in which you want your horse to work the cow. I personally prefer a smaller area than that. I think that even the 180° area offers bad working angles for most horses. From there, they cannot successfully challenge or stop a cow. For me, working between 45° on one side and 135° on the other is a safe working area. Although others may prefer the larger area, I prefer to work in this area.

At any rate, when turning from one side to another, you do not want your horse to over-rotate, or exceed the 180° work area. Should the horse over-rotate, he will turn farther than the 180° imaginary line. If he does this, then he has lost sight of the cow, and he is no longer in position to challenge the cow. This gives the cow plenty of opportunity to return to the herd, since she now has the advantage. The horse is no longer in control and can be pushed back to the corner of the herd.

The problem of over-rotation might be caused by having your angle wrong while working the cow. Your plane might be angled incorrectly. For example, while you are going to the right, you may be up into the cow too much, at an approximate 75° angle, rather than a 45° angle. This is the start of your over-rotation, although the over-rotation itself is going to occur on the turn to the left.

When your horse completes his turn to the left, he will turn more than the 180° plane from your imaginary line

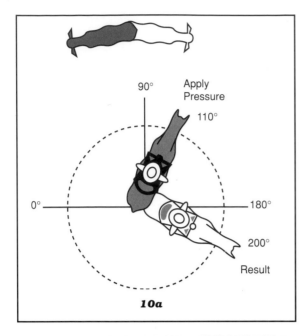

(top) 10a—There is an imaginary plane across the pen on which you work that horse. Turning past that plane is called over-rotation.

(above) Because the horse has over-rotated, he is now too flat and not up into the cow. This has caused a loss of interest.

(previous pages) When a horse over-rotates, meaning he turns more than 180° while working a cow, he has lost sight of the cow and lost his working advantage.

across the pen, over-rotating to approximately 200° to 220°. When this happens, he is giving the cow plenty of opportunity to get away from him. Therefore, he is probably going to lose the cow. If he does not lose her at that turn, a second problem is already in the making. He will most likely run her off now because as he turns around, instead of being at her head or shoulder during his turn, he will be angled at her tail. This will encourage her to run off.

Working an incorrect angle on a cow and facing up to a cow are two different things. Facing up to the cow after stopping means that the horse looks at the cow with both eyes, putting pressure on that cow to control her. I like a horse to do this. I like him to face the cow after he has made his stop.

On facing up to a cow, a horse works on the invisible plane. If my horse does rotate to 180° on the plane, then I immediately want him to close that gap by facing back up to a 45° to 90° angle, only after the horse has completed the stop. I encourage this step after every move, no matter if we are working the cow in the middle of the pen or on the side of the pen. Remember we are not working a pattern, we are working a cow. However, to track across the pen correctly with a cow, you are going to have to line back out to either 0° or 180°. Otherwise, you would be going up into the cow in a "V" position.

When you are working a cow, you start from the middle of the cow (also called "inside the cow") and work to the outside. When I work to the outside I prefer to make smaller turns because smaller turns are safer. At the most, I want no larger than 90° turns. There will be times when working the cow that my horse may be required to make more than 90° turns, but the turns that I can control I keep at 90° or smaller.

To narrow that V-shaped working area, I change my working angle. To do this, I press the horse with my cow-side leg as he is making a turn. Press with the left leg or foot any time *after* the horse has started the turn to the right or vice-versa if going the other direction. This action will cause the turn on the next side to be a little shorter. I have, therefore, narrowed my working area, which will make for safer turns and provide less opportunity for over-rotation.

The best method to correct an over-rotation is to prevent it from happening. Using the cow-side rein, hold your horse up toward the cow when he is turning. If the head stays on the cow and the body continues to over-rotate, you must then stop the horse and change your angle. Or, as you hold the head to the cow, kick the rib with the herd-side leg. This keeps him from rotating any farther than the invisible plane.

A hot-blooded horse is one that will have a tendency to over-rotate because he is a horse that likes to make quick moves. If you feel him about to over-rotate, then pick up on him and slow down his turn. Use very little leg pressure on a hot-blooded horse. He will think you are trying to make him more aggressive. This is exactly the opposite of what you want to do with a hot-blooded horse.

A horse that scrambles, or hits the ground many times while making a turn, will often over-rotate because his momentum will carry him through the turn. Scrambling is caused by not moving the front end correctly, so this is another example of the domino effect. The problem of not moving the front end correctly (problem #1) causes scrambling (problem #2), which, in turn, causes the horse to over-rotate (problem #3) which then causes the horse to lose control of the cow (problem #4).

Timing is essential to rotation. An over-rotation can be man-made. Should you use leg pressure too early when encouraging your horse through a turn, you will shove him up into the cow. You can also create the shoulder turning or rib turning first, which is exactly opposite of what you want. Never use a leg until the turn has been initiated by the horse or by the rider in some instances. When you shove him up into the cow on one side, it is going to change his angle and make him over-rotate on the other side. Likewise, not using leg pressure early enough in some instances can allow a horse to get too flat.

A horse is going to get flat tracking across the pen. I don't want my horse to fall off the cow unless he is trying to release some pressure. If we have a fast cow, my horse can fall off to some degree to help slow her down. Let the horse rotate off the cow more than normal in that instance. Then come back up when the cow has slowed down by encouraging your horse through a turn with your cow-side leg. You can get this done by body movements.

I work to teach a horse to speed up and slow down according to my body tension and relaxation. For example, when you push your weight and hips down in the bottom of the saddle and put pressure in your stirrups, your different levels of intensity will tell your horse to slow down or to stop.

Over-rotation can cost you a cutting. Narrowing down your working field will help eliminate over-rotation, but this is an area where you have to use common sense. To train in a narrow working field, you will have to take your horse off being flat on a cow and stop him, then rock him back a step or two. I am continually pulling him back up into a cow after completing a stop. I don't allow the horse to stay in a flat position but keep him up into that cow at some point. We are talking about a cow that we can control. This maneuver is called pulling him back up into a cow. When you turn him into the cow, you can encourage him to step up into the cow to increase the intensity. Your working area can depend on your horse's physical ability and even on the cattle. For the majority of the time though, I prefer my working field to be in the area of a V with my horse facing the cow.

The horse has over-rotated to the right. Bill slows the rotation down with the left rein, holding the head toward the cow. He will stop the head first and then the body.

11

Working Around Conformation Problems

If there is a problem with your horse, the first thing you should do, as I stated in Chapter Two, is to stop and think things through. Then, after you have grasped that the horse does indeed have a particular problem, decide if it is fixable. Sometimes problems can be corrected, sometimes they can only be improved on and sometimes it is necessary to find ways to work around the problems. Conformation problems often fall into the last category.

GROWING PAINS

Common sense should be the bottom line for all training programs; and if a problem cannot be fixed, then common sense should tell you to figure a way around it. An example of this might be the young horse that still lacks coordination. This is common with young horses and often causes some of their inconsistency in performance. Maybe he is gangly and can't seem to control his legs quite right yet. The horse knows what you want him to do and he tries to do it, but he can't put it all together because he doesn't have complete control of his body. Spanking him because he isn't doing what you want him to do will not solve the problem because physically he can't do it. So rather than constantly harping on the maneuver, work on teaching him to use his body and every once in a while, throw a maneuver in.

You do this by consistently bringing him back and putting him in front of that cow. Every time he makes a move, bring him back after the move so that he is in front of the cow. If he gets tangled up with his legs, or he cannot grasp how to move his front end, just keep bringing him back to that cow. As the opportunity arises, assist him through the maneuver that you want him to do, but do not spank him for not being able to do it at this point. Continu-

Always bring an uncoordinated, young horse back in front of the cow. Even if he gets tangled up with his legs, bring him back to that cow. The horse is mentally trying to please. Although he can not physically perform the maneuver, you continue to teach rather than punish him.

(previous pages) Slowing your training program down is one of the best ways to help your horse work through problem areas.

ally doing this will help him learn coordination, which will help him to correctly make the maneuver.

If you remember when you first learned to dance, your teacher moved smoothly, and even though you knew where to go, you moved awkwardly. It's the same way with the young horse. You are the teacher and he is the pupil. This is an example of a limitation that causes problems, but not forever, so you must work around it for awhile. Just allowing him time to outgrow the inconsistency, plus constant practice, will probably take care of the problem.

Another possible growth problem is the horse that is too high in the hindquarters. Usually, a horse's hindquarters grow first and then his front end catches up. So, if he is in a growth spurt, this might cause his front end to drop lower to the ground than you would want it as you train him. Again, time and maturity will help alleviate this problem.

102

QUICK-MATURING HORSES

Another time that you have to work around limitations is almost exactly opposite the uneven growth problem. Sometimes a horse's physical abilities mature quicker than his mental abilities. You have to be cautious with a real strong horse, especially in his early career because he often tries to do more physically than he is capable of mentally. In the early stages of training, a real physical horse can be frightened easily. Because of his physical ability, and maybe because of eagerness also, he does things so hard and quick that he continually puts himself under stress and makes mistakes. This is another area where you don't try to correct the mistakes, but instead, you work around them. Ignore the mistake. The mistake is a result of the stress from moving too hard and fast.

Instead, help him learn that he can slow down and still handle the cow. Pick a slow cow to work, then keep your horse in a slow trot. Let him learn that he can handle the cow without having to make big, physical moves. When he learns that it is not necessary to go fast on his own, he will correct a lot of the mistakes that he was making.

THE IMPERFECT BUILD

There are certain structural problems that cause working problems and you need to go around them. If you have a horse that is consistently getting on his front end, there may be some physical problems causing this. A horse that constantly gets on his front end, also referred to as "heavy on the front end," is a horse that puts too much weight on his front legs. All horses stand with most of their weight on their front legs. However, a horse that is heavy on his front end stands with a disproportionate amount of weight there, mainly due to conformation faults or soreness in the hindquarters. The latter is usually due to poor conformation in the hindquarters.

You may have a horse that is not balanced in his conformation and stands behind himself a little bit. This means that he stands stretched out behind, which puts too much pressure on his back, stifles, and hocks. This kind of horse may have a tendency to cripple himself. Even if he succeeds in being a good cutting horse, he won't be a real strong stopper because of his weak hindquarters. You will have to work around the problem. The best thing to do is to cut cattle that will help to keep him out of situations where he needs to stop hard.

Another example of an imperfect build is a horse that is not only taller in the hindquarters, but also real long in the underline, which can make him stand out behind himself. Such a horse is not real strong behind, either. When he starts to turn around, he wants to run, scrambling with his front feet. He thinks that's the only way he can do it. The answer is to make him feel secure in the turn by supporting him. You help him keep the turn as controlled as it can be. As he gets older, it is possible he might outgrow some of this, but not all of it.

When you have a horse with the type of conformational

Trotting at a controlled pace allows time for the horse to think and react without cow pressure. When he learns that it is not necessary to go fast, he will correct many of the mistakes that he was making.

problems mentioned above, you have to compensate in your training program. Such a horse cannot physically do what you would like him to do. In working with these problems, cut a slow cow so you can move the horse outside the cow and bring him back. You want to do this a lot because this will help the horse get broke to the cow and keep him wanting to come back. To hold him all of the time would cause some resistance, so you want to step him outside the cow and bring him back. This will help him relax. You also want to be deliberate with things you do. There are no shortcuts, everything must be decisive.

The reason you extend him at first is that at some point in his career he will be outside a cow, and you don't want him to be totally frightened by it. Therefore, in order to teach him to be smart, you must allow him to make mistakes, that is be out beyond the cow.

After you have accomplished this, you change your objective and likewise your training method. You must start teaching him to be just as smart about a cow as he can be. This is done by having him face up to a cow—develop him as being a real pretty show horse, instead of a real physical-type horse. Now, help him stay on the inside of the cow when working by having him make small moves instead of big ones. You never want to continually extend a horse like this with large, sweeping moves that cause the horse to really use his hindquarters. If you over-ride such a horse, you create a problem because he is not physically capable of handling big moves. Keep him collected and teach him about handling a cow.

Sometimes you have to compensate for certain conformation problems. Here Bill is stepping the horse beyond or outside the cow. This will help the horse get broke to the cow. He will learn to relax and will want to come back to the cow.

A horse like this, incapable of one large move after another, has to be deliberate with every step he takes. Every step has to have a purpose and you have to use authority to relay to him that this is the only way he can successfully cut a cow. With horses like these, the more broke you get them, the better the chances you have of getting them shown.

ACCENTUATE THE POSITIVE

I do not believe that you must have a true athlete to win a cutting. In fact, you will probably have a smarter horse if you don't have a real athletic horse. You know the problems a horse has and you have to keep him out of trouble if possible; so you train the horse with problems to be smart.

There is a Smart Little Lena mare that I have won a lot on; yet she was not extremely athletic. She was just so smart about a cow and so trainable, and developed such a pretty style that these three assets made her successful in both the open and the non-pro divisions.

A non-athletic horse can have trouble picking up his front end. If you spend all of your time helping him pick up his front end, the only thing you will accomplish is making his moves more mechanical, instead of natural. Again, common sense is the answer to a good training program. You can't become obsessed about things that just aren't working. You have got to think about what the end product needs to be, which is a trained cutting horse.

If you work on trying to pull that horse up all of the time when that is not something that he can physically do, then you have lost sight of your end product. Instead, find those maneuvers that the horse does well and work to enhance them. By working on his positive traits you will minimize the negative one. If he has trouble dropping his front end, maybe you need to keep him facing up to a cow more, which helps alleviate the need for the front-end movement. Try to take the pressure off him. Cut slow cattle which will keep him from having to run and turn, thus putting him in situations where he has to drop his front end.

Accentuating the positive holds true in all training situations. If your horse can't run, but he shimmies down in front of a cow and looks pretty, then try to cut slow cattle that allow him to stay in the middle of the pen and do this. If it is natural for him to stop hard, then try to cut cattle that are fast, allowing him to run and do his hard, pretty stops. The point is that you don't look at the petty problem. Don't destroy his confidence by making him do something he can't. You will frustrate him and yourself as well. You can spend your entire time picking on little things and then lose sight of the big picture—what that end product really should be.

Remember that your program is to develop a competitive cutting horse, and to do this there are areas you'll have to work around. I refuse to allow myself to look at the little problems. Instead, I keep the whole picture in mind. If I looked only at the little problems, then I would probably ruin a horse by trying to fix one little thing that I could easily learn to work around.

12

Problems with the Front End

I divide horses into halves when discussing them—the front end and the back end. Some of the most common problems that you will run across in your training program involve the horse's front end—his head, shoulders, and front two legs.

GIVING YOU HIS HEAD

Getting your horse to give you his head refers to his willingness to perform the maneuvers that you want him to and not resist you. When you do encounter resistance, the first thing you should ask yourself is "why?"

Did you rush him through a move, which scared him, and automatically made him resist you? If so, slow the working process down for a few minutes and let him relax. Is he too green to mentally handle what you just asked him to do? If that is a possibility, then you have instilled some fear in him, which is making him resist you. Again, just back away from training for a few minutes and let the horse relax.

When you return to your program, go slowly with him and always bring him back to the cow after a move so that he will soon identify coming back to the cow as a security area. It is always better to try to out-think a horse, rather than use brute force to correct a problem.

Could he possibly be sore? Feel all over his body to see if he reacts to pressure. If so, then the soreness is probably causing him to resist you. Continuing to work a horse that is sore might cause a more serious problem and prolong the horse's recovery. Also, a horse that is working in pain is not going to pay attention to your training program, so it is best to stop the training completely and treat the soreness.

Every problem of resistance can be overcome if approached in an intelligent manner. Brute force and intimi-

(previous pages) This horse is completely out of balance due to problems with his front end. He is using his head and neck to maintain his balance and pull himself through the turn.

dation are not the answers. Instead, you need to use finesse.

For example, I once had a little mare that did not want to give me her head. She was not frightened and neither was she sore. She was stiff and just wanted to resist me, so I dry-worked her a little to help her relax. As mentioned in earlier chapters, this is the process of stepping a horse across a cow left and right without the cow really moving.

I soon realized from this maneuver that her resistance was a combination of being a little fresh and having a heavy bit in her mouth. She had not been worked for three days. Since she was just being uncooperative, I needed to be firm with her and get her mind back on the training program. Also, I had put a different bit in her mouth for the first time. The new bit was heavier than what she had been used to having in her mouth. She was probably a little frightened, so she resisted it.

I could have used brute force and jerked on her and made her give me her head, but that would have just made her mad or confused and scared her even more. If this happened, it would not to be easy to have a good training session since her mind would be on her anger and not on learning.

Instead, I tried a different approach to get her to give me her head. I got her thinking about the cow, which took her mind off the bit. This also took care of some of that freshness. I did this by using little tugs or bumps on the reins just to control the momentum as she completed a turn. The little tugs did not actually stop her, but they kept making her control her momentum and also pay attention.

When encountering resistance from your horse, focus his mind on the cow. Use tugs or bumps on the reins and use your feet for motivation to make him pay attention to the cow.

When you are working with resistance, remember to use your feet. Your feet can help you out just as much, and sometimes even more than your hands can. With your hands, you should give the horse directions, such as tugging or bumping on the reins to check him, releasing to let him go, pulling with the left rein to turn left, or pulling with the right rein to turn right.

Your feet provide motivation. For example, when you apply pressure to a horse's side with one foot, that pressure should aid the horse's body through the turn. If you press with both feet at the same time, you are motivating the horse to go forward. You certainly do not want to do that in a turn unless you are too close to the herd and you need to get up out of the herd. At that time you would use any means available to relieve the pressure of the herd from the horse. If it is both feet, then so be it. Otherwise, in a turn, I prefer to use the cow-side foot. For example, turning left, after the turn has started, I use my right foot. I use my left hand for direction and my right foot for pressure.

Timing is important here in a turn. Time things so that you utilize your foot during the turn and not after the turn is completed. If you have a horse that is totally resisting giving you his head, then he needs a little extra motivation. You kick him rather than press him during the turn.

With the little mare I mentioned above, just as soon as I got her to give me her head, I immediately stepped her up to the cow so she had to start thinking about the cow and forget about me correcting her resistance. The action of stepping her up to the cow naturally made the cow move. Since she knew this, her mind was on that cow and she tried to figure out which way the cow was going to move. When the cow moved, she knew which way she needed to go.

Sometimes you get resistance in the early months of training a 2-year-old that has been on cattle 30 to 40 times. When this happens, re-think your program, and see if you are working that young horse too much. You need to spend some time riding him before and after you work. With a 2-year-old you will spend time in the pasture, lope-track or pen just riding before you actually do your cow work. Although each horse is different, in general you can spend 45 minutes to an hour before working him and maybe that much time after as well.

A young horse's mind has a short attention span. Working the cow needs to be fun; the horse needs to be inquisitive about it. When you pressure the young horse by working him too long, it won't be fun anymore and he will start resisting you.

HORSE FALLING ON HIS HEAD

The term "falling on his head" refers to the manner in which a horse makes a turn. When a horse is falling on his head, he is not turning in a balanced manner. I refer to it this way, since this is what it looks like he is doing in the turn. He is allowing all of his weight to be placed on his front end for some reason. Another common term is being "heavy on the front end." The problem could be the fault of his

Your feet provide motivation. Encouraging the horse with the left foot should aid the horse's body through the turn.

This horse has "fallen on his head." He needs to be slowed down and rocked back to compensate for his eagerness to turn before completing the stop.

(above) To correct falling on the head, catch the horse in his stop, rock him back, then pick up his front end.

(opposite top) To correct a shoulder-first turn, Bill completely stops the horse and balances his body. He pushes the horse's shoulder underneath the horse with his cow-side leg.

(opposite bottom) Bill braces the horse's head and stops the shoulder movement with his foot.

conformation, or it could be man-made and relate to the way he stops or doesn't stop.

If falling on his head is not a physical problem for the horse, as discussed in Chapter 11, then it can often be corrected. To fix the problem, I would rock the horse back to help him learn to take his weight off his front end. I don't like to back a horse a whole lot because this can create another problem. Continually backing the horse can cause him to become rigid and stiff. But backing him a little will help him learn to shift the weight from the front end to the back end. Back him a few steps, just enough so that you know he has learned to take the weight off of his front end. Then, pick up his front end.

Let's begin with a right turn. Take the right rein in your right hand and the left rein in your left hand. You will use them independently of one another. With the right hand, lead the horse with his nose coming first through a turn. Now after the turn is complete, using both hands simultaneously pull him to a firm stop, pulling him down into the ground. At the same time signal him with your body movements to stop.

Do not let go of your stop too quickly. You want to pull the horse into the stop so that he places his weight on his hindquarters. He learned how it felt to place his weight on his hindquarters during your backing maneuvers. When he gets his weight on his back end, it will be easier for him to pivot or move his weight left or right.

After he has stopped completely, then take the left rein and use some right leg to move his body out and across the cow, pulling the horse's nose to a turn to the left. Again, after completing the turn, use both reins to help him stop by pulling him down into the ground, as you push your body weight down in the saddle. To accomplish this, collapse your shoulders straight down, not leaning back toward the hip of the horse, but collapsing the small of your back and your shoulders straight down. Put added pressure to the pockets of your jeans. This should put his weight on his back feet. Patiently repeat the scenario time and time again until you feel that the horse is understanding what you want him to do and you have gotten some control.

MOVING THE HEAD BACK AND FORTH

The habit a horse may have of moving his head back and forth is irritating more than anything else. Always check first to make sure that nothing is bothering your horse—the bridle is on correctly; there is nothing wrong with the bit; horse flies are not agitating his head, etc. Then, take hold of his head lightly with your reins and just hold him there for several minutes before releasing him. Try repeating this several times.

Should this form of correction not solve his head moving, take hold of him lightly, as before, for a few seconds and pull him around with authority. Then put him back on the cow. Always give him something to do with the cow. An idle horse will sometimes become bored so you want to remain aggressive with your teaching process.

COMING WITH THE SHOULDER

"Coming with the shoulder" refers to an incorrect way that a horse turns. If he allows his shoulder to move into the turn before his head and neck initiate the turn, then he is coming with his shoulder first. If a horse leads through that turn with his shoulder first rather than the head and neck, then he is pushing his shoulder out so that it is the first part of his body to start turning. When he does this, he is unbalanced and not flowing through his moves. Chances are, he is going to drop his front end or rotate up into the cow, thus hitting the cow in the hip and chasing or running her off. This is generally followed by a choppy front end.

To correct a shoulder-first turn, I gather the horse by holding both reins steady to brace the horse's head and to balance his body. I want a complete stop before I start the correction. Then, I push his shoulder back underneath him with my cow-side foot. I do this through leg pressure. I don't jab the horse with my foot. In other words, I press his shoulder with my foot that is closest to the cow. I don't kick him in the shoulder with my spur. Then, I balance him once again by gathering him for another stop.

To summarize this technique, I brace the horse's head, which helps him turn correctly. I stop the shoulder movement with my foot, and I encourage the nose movement with the pull of the reins.

The horse should begin to make the move correctly by himself. However, if we are in the early stages of training, I continue to help him bring his nose first by encouraging the turn with the appropriate rein. For example, the right rein for a right turn and the left rein for a left turn. At the same time I am pulling the nose and stepping the horse through the turn, I rock him back, not only with the indirect rein but also with the rein that is giving direction until the turn is initiated. Then, the pressure is released and the rein hand that is giving direction picks up and leads through the turn and the indirect rein becomes dormant. I am rocking the horse back with both reins, then the direct rein starts pulling the nose through the turn and giving direction. The other rein gives and takes to maintain that backward pressure on the horse until the turn is initiated; otherwise, I am just circling up into the cow.

Sometimes, when the horse is really trying for me but turns badly with the cow, even though he has been corrected several times for this, I will just ride him through the turn. I do this because I do not want him to feel like he is going to be punished every time he does things incorrectly. I want him to keep his mind on the cow and not on me. Should I correct him every time he takes a step, before long he will have his mind on me and what I might do to him next, rather than on the cow.

Deciding what to do about every problem is not as simple as black and white. Often it requires a judgment call on your part. For example, one horse I had turned through his right-hand turn really well, but when he turned back to his left, he pushed his shoulder out and this caused him to raise up a bit in that left-hand turn. I decided that I would

(previous pages) *Overhead views effectively illustrate 'coming with the shoudler.' Both horses come through the turn with their shoulders first.*

not make a big deal out of it because I believed this problem would take care of itself within the year as the horse developed more intensity on cattle. Therefore, I made the judgment call to live with a little bit of a problem in order to get the overall picture.

Another horse I had, a mare, would start through her left-hand turn by elevating herself and trying to come with her shoulder before she turned her head and neck. To correct her, I stepped her farther to the right, or over-rotated to the right, before I allowed her to start her stop. I did this on a real slow cow, so I didn't scare her.

This extension gave me more time to work with her shoulder and her head. It gave me the time to pull her nose through that turn first, which helped her make the turn correctly. Once she was making the turn correctly, she had time to complete the turn and still come with the cow, although she was extended.

If I hadn't extended her to the right as a method of helping her place the shoulder correctly, when she pushed through that turn to the left, she would have gone through the turn too far—a problem of over-rotating.

The normal reaction would have been to shut her down over on the left. But this usually doesn't solve the problem because her momentum coming from the right is causing her to over-rotate. It is just a reaction to the incorrect turn. Trying to correct the over-rotation until the right side is corrected would have confused her and led to more problems.

However, when I corrected her problem of elevating and trying to come with her shoulder on the right side, it stopped her from pushing through the turn too far on the left.

PUSHING WITH THE RIB CAGE

A horse cannot turn around with his nose first when his ribs are pushed out toward the cattle. Instead, the ribs get in the way and he will turn with his shoulder first, rather than his nose first. I want a horse to follow his nose around. I complete the stop and start the process of rocking back to face up to the cow. If his ribs are in the way, we cannot rock back and face up.

For example, say the horse is parallel to the cow with his left rig cage pushed toward the cow. It will be difficult, if not impossible, for him to turn to the left with his nose first if the cow makes a sudden move to the horse's left. First, I gather him up to give him security and direction. Then I bump his nose towards the cow or rock him back, but at the same time I have a hold of his head to give him the security, and start rocking him back to press that leg. This is a young horse. Later, with a more advanced horse, you can just put a little leg pressure with your foot or leg, or even the spur, to get him to look at the cow and then the run continues.

Here, however, we are correcting the head for security and direction and then deal with the rib. To do this, we go back to the basics. Rock him back, get everything back underneath you and then face him back up to the cow. Here is where you can step that horse across the cow and do a little dry work to get that rib underneath him, to get everything back in line, to get that balance, to get control. Then you face back up to the cow and the run continues.

That is why I use a lot of cow-side foot to put pressure on the rib cage. If I use the cow-side foot to push back the rib cage to its proper position in the middle of the horse's body, I can make the horse's head come toward the cow. I am not using the foot to accelerate, but rather to bend the horse into the cow.

I prefer not to jab a horse at first. I try to correct this problem by rolling the spur up the horse's side. If I don't get results, then I will jab him. However, that is the last resort.

I try to avoid pain and punishment situations as much as possible. When I use my foot and don't get the head to come like I want it to come with the cow, then I slide my hand down the cow-side rein and bump the horse's nose toward the cow. Once you have the head in the right direction, then you can come with one foot at a time. I may alternate those feet when I drive toward the cow but seldom will I use both feet at the same time for any reason. This will center the horse on the cow so he is not flat—not too parallel to the cow—and so he doesn't have to make a big move.

SCRAMBLING THROUGH A TURN

If your horse scrambles through a turn, he is not making a flowing movement with his front end. Scrambling is when the horse takes several little steps to get himself turned around with the cow. He is not flowing when he is scrambling. The turn is more difficult for him, and it usually places him behind the cow in the run.

If a horse is turning to the right and does not make the complete axis of a turn from one side to another, he is leaving his front end up in the cow and not moving it across the cow to complete the turn. This causes him to be unbalanced, which will then create a problem on the turn to the left. He'll either fade off or over-rotate as he turns to the left.

To correct this, line him out a little bit farther on the right-hand side by holding the right rein out and not allowing him to turn to the left too soon. In doing this you are not extending him and getting flat, but rather rotating him a little bit farther to the right. Next, press and roll your spur up his rib or shoulder on the left-hand side to get him through the turn to the right. This will also help him maintain balance and prepare him to stop.

Once you get his body, head, and neck turning to the right, use the left rein to keep his nose tipped toward the cow, which keeps him from rotating too far to the right. This is an exaggerated movement to free his front end up and get him moving smoothly.

13

Other Specific Problems

Most problems cannot be fixed one time and then forgotten. Working a horse through a problem area requires a lot of slowing down, sitting, and waiting. It may take session after session after session to cure a problem, especially if you let it get too far out of hand. In fact, during your everyday training program, you will need to constantly correct mistakes that your horse is making. The horse needs to relate to what you are doing to him. You make one turn at a time rather than multiple turns, you slow down, you back off, you let your horse think. To do otherwise may create more problems than you already have.

LEAKING

When a horse is leaking he is driving a cow when he shouldn't be. The reason he is leaking is that he has not completed his stop before the turn. Most of the time this is caused by rider reaction. The rider who uses his body to try to initiate a turn, as opposed to initiating a stop first, can create this overbalance and pull a horse up into a cow, thereby losing the stop.

Occasionally, an older horse gets show smart and will start leaking under show conditions. When that happens, all the work at home may not stop it. You are going to have to correct this horse under show conditions and let him know that he is going to have to complete his stops and be crisp in a turn. You correct this problem by forcing the horse to complete the stop before initiating the turn.

TURNING BEFORE STOPPING

I always want my horse to make a clean stop before he starts to make a turn. When a horse moves his hindquarters away from the cow just before he makes his stop, he is trying

(above) When a horse moves his hindquarters away from the cow before stopping, he is trying to turn before he has completed the stop.

(right) Should you recognize that your horse is trying to cheat you in his turns, exert control with the reins to prevent him from turning too quickly.

(previous pages)   The ultimate objective in a training program is a horse that is in sync with the cow and moves in a precise rhythmic manner.

to turn, rather than stop and then turn. It makes no difference if your horse is turning to the right or to the left, you want him to complete his stop before he begins his turn.

In the next chapter on "Body Position", I discuss how turning before completing a good stop can be a man-made problem. The rider does not have faith in his horse to turn in time, so he drops his shoulder and leans as if to turn himself. This signals the horse to turn before he has completed his stop, and throws the horse off balance.

However, if this is not the problem and you are sitting correctly, then the horse is cheating you by starting to turn before he stops. First, you might try bumping him with the bit as he starts into the ground to remind him to stop before he turns. If this does not solve the problem, then stop him from starting the turn by pulling back firmly with both reins. After bringing the horse to a complete stop, rock him back a step or two, and then help him start the turn correctly. This technique will keep him straight and not allow him to start turning early. Only after you get a good stop do you allow your horse to proceed with the turn.

Exerting control with the reins keeps the horse from turning too quickly. Your body movements (previously discussed) can also encourage your horse to come to a clean stop. Hopefully, the combination of the reins and the clean stop will help solve the problem. The main thing is to recognize in the early stages that your horse is trying to cheat you in his turns. You don't want him to do this

because when a horse turns without stopping, he is likely to get behind the cow. His run will soon look like he is making figure 8s in the arena, which will also make him harder to ride.

FALSE MOVES

A false move occurs when a horse anticipates or reacts to a move that the cow did not make. It is a move that is not coordinated with a cow—a response on the horse's part that the cow did not initiate. The horse usually moves side-to-side with his front feet when he anticipates.

There are two kinds of horses that make false moves: the horse that reads the situation incorrectly, and the mechanical horse. Misreading the situation often happens. Generally, there is not much you can do about this. Most of the time, the physically active horse is the type that reads the cow wrong and makes an error. He's a horse that thinks a lot on his own and just flat reads the cow wrong in anticipation of the cow's move. Perhaps he is an aggressive horse, one that got a little overanxious, and instead of focusing on the cow and moving with the cow, he just made phantom moves.

If the horse is hyperactive and makes false moves, you can slow him down in the training pen, which will help control this. Working with him slowly in the training pen helps him relax and build confidence. He'll realize he doesn't need to move so fast; but it is no sure-fire cure for eliminating the false moves under show conditions. Your main objective is to establish more control in the training pen, which should then help you in the show arena.

The other kind of horse that makes false moves is the mechanical horse. This horse is not working a cow. Instead, most of the time he is working a pattern or moving just for the sake of moving because he is told to do so by his rider. Some people prefer to have this much control over the horse. They can cut a dead cow that doesn't move and just push the buttons. I do not want mechanics in my horses.

I prefer to move a horse toward a cow, not side-to-side in front of a cow. When I encourage my horse to move toward the cow, he soon learns that this will cause the cow to move. I also use this technique when I have a horse that squirms around a lot in front of a cow. It is his way of resisting, of showing his nervous energy. He knows that when the cow moves, she has got to go somewhere. So I go ahead and make this happen. I put the horse up into the cow and force the cow to go somewhere, which then gives the horse something to do.

My other alternative to this is to totally restrict the horse from making any moves. But, if I do this, I might take that cowiness away from him. Since I am trying to encourage him to read the cow, pay attention to her, and move with her, I feel that my avenue of escape is to give him something else to do, rather than trying to stop him from squirming. You can move the horse straight up into the cow with either foot or both. Ultimately, the horse will turn that nervous energy into a winning performance because he will start squatting

into the ground instead of squirming. In anticipation of the cow's move, he will start lowering himself into the ground, in a creeping motion. This is a fairly dramatic move and looks good in the show pen.

FALLING OFF OF A COW—LOSING GROUND

When a horse is falling off of a cow, or losing ground, it means that he is moving away from that cow as the two go across the pen. He puts more room between himself and the cow with each step he takes. To correct this problem, pick up the cow-side rein and hold your horse as you go across the pen so that he can not angle away from the cow. In other words, hold him up to the cow. The herd-side rein will put pressure across the horse's neck, keeping the head turned toward the cow and the body straight. The horse we are talking about here is a 3-year-old or older and we are already using a little neck-rein on him.

When he comes back through his next turn, he should stay in the desired working area. Also, as you are coming out of your turn before starting across the pen again, use your cow-side leg immediately when you come out of the turn to hold your horse up into the cow. Press or spur and release. (Caution: do not hold the spur or your leg on the horse. That would cause the horse to think more about the spurring or leg pressure than the cow.) This will help to hold his head toward the cow, rather than allow him to move his head away from the cow. It will also help maintain that parallel line coming across the pen. These corrections will stop him from being up into a cow too much.

Another option is to give the horse a change of scenery. Perhaps changing the horse to the square pen will help mend the problem. The square pen provides a straighter working line and does not offer as much opportunity as the round pen for your horse to fall off the cow.

Cow fear, whether it is caused by the rider, the cattle, or the pen, is the usual reason for a horse falling off a cow. Pens are largely responsible for this problem. There will always be a spot in every pen which puts the most pressure on your horse. At the Will Rogers Coliseum in Fort Worth, for

(left) **This horse is in an ideal position to challenge the cow.**

(opposite) **When a horse makes false moves, Bill likes to move the horse toward the cow instead of side-to-side. This forces the cow to go somewhere and gives the horse the chance to respond.**

example, that spot is on the left-hand side about three-quarters of the way across the pen.

So, changing pens may solve your problem. You can take your horse back to the 60 x 60-foot pen where you work with only one cow and really take the pressure off the horse, allowing him time to relax and once again adjust to the cow. Or maybe just changing to the 90 x 90-foot square pen for the straighter line will fix the problem. You can even go to a larger round pen and let the horse return to the basic technique of reading a cow and then trapping her. This takes the pressure off the horse also. Of course, if you are going to return to using these basic methods, which is like returning to "square one," then you must have enough time in your training program to allow for working back through the program.

If, on the other hand, you are up against a show deadline, then you need to go to the square pen and fix the falling off problem. There, you will be working the straighter line and most likely working with less cattle than in the round pens. Find a slow cow to work since that will also eliminate pressure on the horse.

LEANING ON A COW

The direct opposite of falling away from a cow is leaning toward a cow. This means that the horse goes across the pen angling his body just a little toward the cow in an attempt to make the cow run off. When he does this, he is not drawing the cow, rather he is pushing the cow, even though he may not be noticeably stepping or moving toward the cow. It is almost an invisible pressure, but it is a pushing action toward the cow which is contradictory to the drawing that you desire, and it is uncomfortable to ride. A miss or loss is inevitable.

To correct this problem, bump the reins first to slow the horse down, then use your feet. With slight pressure on the reins to hold the head, bump the rib on the cow-side. This should move the horse away from the pressure. If slight pressure doesn't work, you can then be more aggressive. When going to the right, place your left foot in his shoulder to keep the front end underneath him instead of pushing toward the cow. This maneuver may also be completed by using your left leg in the rib and contact on the reins. You may release the foot pressure when you get the correct response. But don't forget to release the pressure that you have on the shoulder or rib when you get to the stop. This is a press and release maneuver. If I need to come back to that, then I will do so. You could also attempt to speed the horse up which will cause him to have some type of reaction from the cow. Most of the time, you will force him to make a commitment to the cow and the cow to him, which will create a stop and a turn. Sometimes this added cow pressure will enhance the performance and correct the leaning on the cow. By the same token, you may even try slowing up, coming back inside of the cow, and letting the cow push you a little. This may help correct the leaning. When you are doing this, you should also maintain light contact with the horse's mouth. This is to secure the horse and/or give him direction.

A third correction that you might try is a simple bump of the bit to re-establish respect and control and then re-direct your horse. Any one of these three corrections, with varying degrees of authority, will help to eliminate the leaning problem.

TOO FLAT

Being too flat on a cow means the horse is at such a parallel line that it will be difficult for your horse to turn around smoothly and in one motion. Your horse will probably be choppy through the turn and may even over-rotate. He could, in fact, lose his working advantage and not be in the position to challenge the cow.

You cannot control a cow by being too flat. It is too difficult for a horse to respond smoothly and with quickness. This horse must be a true athlete to have a chance. In the practice pen, get a slow-moving cow. Then move your horse back and forth with the cow. As you turn from one side to the other, as soon as the horse executes the stop, pull his head back toward the cow so he is looking at her. Then rock him back and face him up to the cow. In other words, bring him bodily back so that he is facing the cow. If the cow takes a step toward you, then encourage your horse to take a step toward the cow. This step by your horse puts him on the offense which will give him confidence and control.

TOO SHORT OR TOO LONG

When the horse is short on a cow, he is not stepping out and attempting to stop or challenge the cow. The actual position of a horse that is short can be anywhere in the area of the cow's body from the neck back to the hip. Extremely short is even farther behind. Stepping out to the head of the cow or a little beyond would be the correct position to challenge a cow.

When the horse is short, the cow has an opportunity to return to the herd. To correct this problem, I ride him a little harder to the side where he stops short. You have to accelerate the horse to get to the point where he should be with the cow's head.

Too short to one individual may not be too short to another. There are some individuals who train horses that far back. These are defensive showmen and trainers and some are very successful in doing this. However, this is my opinion about where I want a horse to be. I train aggressively and I show aggressively.

A horse that is too long is doing the exact opposite of one that is too short. He is taking a step too far before he stops. This also creates a space for the cow to return to the herd. A horse that is too long definitely has a problem. It can be caused by the rider being tricked by the cow, a lack of desire by the horse, or an extremely physical horse over-reacting.

If he has stepped too far to the left, then after he has initiated the turn, I use my left foot to push him back over in front of the cow. You would have to be cautious about

After the horse executes a stop, bring him back so that he is facing the cow. From this position, should the cow take a step toward you, you can encourage your horse to take a step toward the cow.

123

leaving your foot in the horse too long. It is a matter of pressing and releasing. If that doesn't work, use more authority, more pressure. In a training situation, you may have to give direction with your hand while pressing with your foot.

In the majority of cases, when a horse loses a cow on one side of the pen, the loss probably started on the other side. With practice, as you watch horses work, you can see this coming before it happens. Often, before losing the cow, the horse extended himself too far past the cow on the opposite side.

This overextension caused him to turn late, placing him at the cow's hip while coming out of the turn. This encouraged the cow to run. Now the horse ends up chasing the cow to the other side of the pen and losing her.

By the same token, if a horse is too short, a similar situation occurs. For example, if the horse is too short on the right side, it means he is not stepping over far enough in his turn to stop that cow. He will then create a problem on the left side. Too short on the right will mean the horse will end up being too long, or extending too far past the cow, on the left. Basically, he is not working off the center of the cow. When the horse is short, his head is at the cow's hip during a turn rather than turning nose to nose with the cow. Likewise, if he is long, he has extended himself past her head so now his hip is at her head.

Either of these are dangerous situations, since you are allowing room for the cow to duck under your horse and get away. Correcting one side will usually correct the other. Bump the bit right after he rotates through the turn going to the left. This will encourage him to slow down as he comes out of the turn and not over-extend himself. Then ride him a little stronger, encourage him a little more going to the right, which will make him take another step or two and not be short. Remember that when he makes a turn to the left, don't continue riding him hard since that is the side that you are trying to slow down.

STIFFNESS

If, when working your horse, he feels stiff, stop your training program and try to limber or supple him. A stiff horse won't be able to turn well. When he is limber, he will be able to work the cow correctly.

One method I use to limber a horse is to move him in a complete circle pulling his nose toward the inside of the circle. This limbers the neck. Make your circle in both directions so that you are pulling the nose in to the right going one direction and in to the left going the other way. Don't use a steady pull. Use a give-and-take motion; just move your fingers. Don't hold the bridle reins with your hands. Hold them with your fingers so you can manipulate them better. Pull on one rein so you can turn the horse's nose a little. Then release it. Steady pressure could make the horse resist and pull back on you. Tugging and releasing will bring his nose in such a fashion that he will walk around in the direction of the pull.

If the rib cage, or the barrel area of the horse, feels a little stiff while doing this, then use your inside leg and just roll the spur up the side. You will get an immediate response and soften up this situation.

Another method to limber your horse is to do dry work. Move your horse back and forth from the left to the right. By this I mean, move your horse out in one direction and stop him; then rock him back over his hocks, tip his nose to the inside, and make him step across himself to change direction. Then trot him out a few steps and do the same thing again until you get some noticeable change in the horse; until you feel he is responding to you.

When you are working a cow and you feel stiffness in your horse, use your legs to help get the horse limber and bending his body. You can accelerate the horse out of the turn with pressure from your cow-side leg. Your acceleration is going to demand some response. He has got to show some suppleness to get back to that cow. By over-riding him, you have the opportunity to correct the problem. After the stop, pull the horse's nose toward the cow. Use quite a bit of pressure from your cow-side leg to get him to bend his body. By pulling the nose and using leg pressure simultaneously, you will create the bend and remove the stiffness.

SLUGGISHNESS

If a horse is sluggish in his turns, you might brighten him up by encouraging him through a turn. As he is turning to his right, use your left foot, which now becomes the cowside foot, and press or roll your spur up his side. If this does not accelerate him, then the next time he makes a turn, stick that spur in his rib cage with authority, but then get out of him. In some instances you can really spur him to accelerate—build a fire under him.

FEAR

Fear will definitely cause a horse to run off. I once had a little sorrel mare that had a light mouth and needed little pressure to get her to respond. If I jerked on her extensively, she would get frightened and have her mind on me rather than the cow. Since she could not concentrate on the training program, she would do numerous things wrong.

To correct this, I first removed the fear that I had caused. I stopped and walked her around a couple of circles to give her time to relax. The next thing to try in a situation like this is a change of equipment. Because she was uptight, I went back to a sidepull for a while, which really let her relax. The next step was to change to a milder bit. This also helped reduce the fear. I could have continued to use the same bit, but in a smoother, softer manner.

The best thing that can happen if you continue to train under fear is that you will just waste time. The worst thing that can happen is the domino effect with mistakes. One mistake will create another mistake which will create another mistake.

"YOUR BODY POSITIONING CAN MAKE OR BREAK YOUR RUN."

14

Body Position

Your body position has a direct impact on how well your horse performs. Because there are a lot of variables involved in cutting, your horse needs a jockey on his back who is going to help and not hinder his task. Whether your horse is running, stopping or turning, you can use your body to help him maximize his run.

BODY WEIGHT

First, always sit in the middle of your horse's back. Sitting heavier on one side of the saddle throws more of your weight to that side. Your weight is now uneven on the horse's back and this gives him an added problem to contend with while he is trying to work the cow. If you sit in the middle of the horse's back, then your weight is distributed evenly in both stirrups.

Leaning creates a similar problem. Some riders have a tendency to lean in their turns. It is the biggest mistake you can make with your body position. If you lean in the direction of the cow when your horse starts to turn, you drop your shoulder toward the direction of the turn. As the horse tries to turn, he finds you in his way. By leaning, you have created a spot that the horse has to get around to complete his turn. Since your weight is leaning toward the cow, the horse will be pulled toward the cow, too, because his body weight will follow yours. He can neither stop nor turn around cleanly.

It is similar to having a child sitting on your shoulders. If the child starts to lean to one side, his body weight will pull you to that side, disturbing your balance. In the same way, when a rider drops his shoulder and leans toward the cow, he disturbs the horse's balance. Since it is now difficult for him to stop and turn, the horse will soon quit trying to do

(previous pages) The rider's hands are working independently of one another. He is providing security with the left hand while leading the nose with the right hand.

(opposite) The rider has correct position on the horse. His heels are down and he is not exerting a great deal of pressure on the stirrups.

(left) When a rider sits heavier on one side of the saddle, his weight is uneven on the horse's back. The rider drops his shoulder, hindering the horse's ability to turn.

this and begin "circling" his turns, causing his run to look like figure 8s.

Problems are like a row of falling dominoes. One wrong move will create another wrong move, which will create another wrong move, and so on. Since your leaning (problem #1) is causing your horse to make circles instead of stopping and turning, (problem #2), this makes him late in coming back with the cow (problem #3). Being late causes him to have to chase her across the pen (problem #4), and then you have a running match which you will lose (problem #5). Notice that this all started because of the rider's incorrect body position. None of this was the horse's fault to begin with and to correct him before you correct yourself will just create confusion.

When the horse is accelerating across the pen, lift your weight out of the saddle or lean forward in the saddle to help him run. In doing this, you are talking to him with your body, encouraging him to run, to go on across the pen. You are also removing dead weight from the center of his back and, therefore, you are making it easier for him to run.

During a stop, using your body correctly can help him make it a clean, crisp stop. To do this, sit down in the saddle; in other words, push down on the seat of your jean pockets with all of your weight. Shifting your weight down into the saddle will cause you to lean back just a little bit. This movement will telegraph to the horse almost the exact spot for him to stop. Since you are pushing down with your body, it will be a whole lot easier for him to push down on his hindquarters. He relies on this help. If you don't do this, then you can cause him to be late with his stop. If you just sit there like dead weight and don't help him to stop, he will have to gather enough power to stop his weight and your weight, too.

Lean forward or lift your weight out of the saddle to help your horse accelerate. Either action will remove dead weight from the center of the horse's back and make it easier for him to run.

(opposite top)   The rider has excellent body position. His head is turning and his shoulders are straight.   He also has a good, straight vertical line from body to leg.

(opposite bottom)   The rider is turning his body before the horse initiates the turn. This throws the horse off balance, impeding his ability to stop or turn around cleanly.

There are exceptions to these rules. Sometimes putting more of your body weight on one side of the horse can help to correct a mistake he is about to make. Timing is an important factor here. Should the horse get excited in his run and try to turn before he makes a clean, crisp stop, the correct body movement from you can help him to make a proper stop.

You can shift your body weight to the herd-side stirrup at the same time you sit down in the saddle to help him stop. By sitting down in the saddle, you are signaling him to stop. Then, by putting more weight on the herd-side stirrup, you are forcing him into the ground a little bit longer because he now has to gather more momentum on that side to turn around. What you are doing by shifting your weight to that side is trying to stop him from turning before he stops. With your body movements, you are stopping what you don't want—the turn before the stop—and encouraging what you do want—the stop and then the turn.

Of course, if your horse makes good, clean, crisp stops and turns and you shift your weight to the herd-side leg, you could cause a problem as easily as you could solve one. The shifting of your weight holds the horse in the ground a little longer. But since he was already making his stops and turns correctly, he doesn't need to do this. Shifting your weight to the herd-side leg could cause him to be late in his turn. By the time he gets out of the turn, he will probably be at the cow's hip, which will run her off. This is pilot error—the horse was doing just fine until his pilot interfered.

Although there are times when it might be beneficial to shift your weight to your herd-side leg, seldom will there be a need to put more of your weight on the cow-side leg. This would be placing an obstacle in the horse's way while turning. He would have to come around your leg in order to complete his turn. Since your weight on the cow-side leg is in the way and hindering his turn, it may cause him to step up into the cow because that would be easier than turning around your leg.

SHOULDERS

Sometimes a rider doesn't trust his horse to stop and turn with the cow. Such a rider leans his body back and also turns his shoulders before the horse has begun the stop and turn. Trying to turn around before the horse stops and turns causes the same problem as dropping your shoulder and leaning toward the cow. You have thrown the horse off balance and you are in his way for the turn.

When you ride your horse correctly through turns, you remain seated in the center of his back. You do not allow your body to get behind what the horse is doing and thus slow him down, or get ahead of what the horse is doing and throw him off balance. Your timing has got to be in sync with the horse's timing. You need to turn with the horse, not before or after him.

If you do not allow the horse to complete the stop before he picks up his front end to move through the turn, then you will often cause the horse to fall on his head. This is a

problem in our industry. The rider sees a turn about to happen and does not have faith in his horse, or the patience to sit still and allow the horse to completely handle the turn. Instead, the rider feels a need to turn right now. He drops his shoulder and bodily starts to turn. A shift in rider body weight throws the horse off balance. Doing this does not give the horse the opportunity to stop and then make the turn. The rider's movements took the stop away from the horse. It made the horse get heavy on the front. He falls on his head during the turn simply because he was not allowed the opportunity to stop.

If you continue to do this, you will inadvertently teach your horse to hurry and possibly fall on his head. Then you will have a big problem. The best thing to do is always pay attention to your body movements so that you can correct this at the very first sign of the problem. Go back to the basics of stopping completely, then prepare and initiate each turn with any problem. Try to slow things down.

LEGS

Just like the shoulders that need to stay in the middle of the horse, your legs need to stay there also, unless you are training or encouraging your horse in some way. Proper leg

and when reining a horse, try to compensate for it with your body. Another suggestion is to reach up and get both reins with both hands and hold the horse straight. By using this method, your body will not have a tendency to lean to one side. Holding the horse with both hands will also help keep him balanced and in a straight line.

SADDLE HORN

Since my left hand holds the reins during competition, I wrap my right hand around the neck of the saddle horn for support. Sometimes, however, I place my right hand on top of the saddle horn. I use the saddle horn differently depending on the horse I am showing. The more athletic horse causes me to wrap my hand around the saddle horn. For the not so athletic one, I place my hand closer to the top or on the top. As with the placement of your rein hand, the placement of your other hand is wherever it is comfortable for that particular horse. For me, the main idea is that I try to adjust to the horse rather than have the horse adjust to me.

If you use it properly, the saddle horn can be a big asset when your horse is working. For example, when he starts into the ground to initiate a turn, then you push against the saddle horn. You are already pushing down into the saddle to help him complete his stop and turn, so pushing against the saddle horn will help keep you balanced.

When the horse steps out of the turn and starts across the pen, then you need to pull on the saddle horn. You can't push when he is coming out of the turn because to do so will shove you out of the saddle. The most important thing is to use your common sense. During practice sessions stop and think about what you are doing. It only makes sense that you can't push on the saddle horn all of the time. There will be times when you have to pull, especially when your horse is accelerating across the pen. By working the saddle horn you can use it to your benefit as a balancing point.

RIDER TENSION

A nervous and tense rider can cause others problems. If you are very nervous and tense, you might find yourself pulling on the saddle horn. If you do that when your horse stops, your weight will jerk forward and this movement will cause you to stand up in your stirrups. You are then interfering with your horse's balance. He now has all of your weight on his front end instead of in the middle of his back, so he is not balanced to execute his turn properly.

Shoulders that are swelled up or humped up also show that a rider is tense. The body language of a rider who sits at the back of the saddle, and leans forward with his shoulders humped, is telling you that he is really tight. The horse is reading this body language also. He feels what the rider does and in this instance he is feeling the rider's tension. Consequently, the horse will become tight and rigid, too, because that is what his rider's tension communicates to him. With this undue stress, the horse's mind is not on cutting the cow. Tension can cause the rider's timing to be off, which can make the horse's timing off, also. Anytime a rider is tight and brings his shoulders up and forward, his horse is naturally going to be out of sync. Again, there will be the domino effect. Problem #1, a tense rider, creates problem #2, a tense horse. In turn, problem #2 creates problem #3, the horse's mind is not on the cow. This furthers problem #4, the rider's and horse's timing are not synchronized.

BEFORE YOU BLAME YOUR HORSE

So often cutting horse competitors buy a horse that is really showing well and winning some checks—the two things he wants the horse to continue to do for him. However, after that person has bought the horse, the horse quits winning. He loses his pretty stop and starts making circles instead, turns into the cow, and sometimes just flat runs away in the show pen.

The competitor wants to know why this winning horse has quit bringing home checks. Since it is obvious that the horse is making mistakes, the first thing the competitor wants to do is blame the horse and discipline him. A lot of good horses have been ruined this way. In reality, the horse is just following the rider's body signals. Although the horse may be doing things wrong, often he is doing them because that is what the rider is telling him to do through his body language.

Before you start blaming your horse, check your body positions. Get someone to video a practice work session so you can see what you are "saying" to your horse. Study that film over and over so that you will be conscious of your body movements and get them corrected. Then buy a video of your performance at shows. Even though you may have corrected some of your body position faults at home, it wouldn't be unusual to see yourself regress a little when you get under the stress of show conditions.

Your body positioning can make or break your run. It has a lot to do with your balance on the horse, which, in turn, helps the horse to maintain his balance while working the cow. It keys right into your timing with his movements, helping to keep everything synchronized. Without good body positioning, you won't have a winning run. Before you start blaming a horse for a bad run, make sure you're not the cause in some way.

For me this is very important because I want to be a vital part of my horse's competitive run. I want to help him while he is working a cow, and I want to let him know that I am with him at all times. I am constantly changing body positions to assist him in moving faster and stopping easier. If you continue to just sit in the saddle and never change your position, no matter what the horse is doing, then you are not communicating anything positive to him through body language. Neither are you providing him with any security or encouragement because you are not giving him signals that you are in the game with him.

15

Tack and Equipment

It is important to have correct, properly fitted equipment, but what that is often depends on the horse. You fit equipment to the individual horse. Your personal likes and dislikes also enter into your decision.

Choice of tack is strictly personal preference. I choose my tack for two reasons: it must suit my training program and be comfortable to use. Since these are the tools of my trade and I use them every day, they must fit my program, fit me, and be a good product.

SADDLE

There is quite a difference between a cutting horse saddle and those used for other western performance sports. Cutting saddles are relatively flat in through the seat, not built up as much in front toward the swells as a pleasure horse, equitation, or roping saddle might be. This gives the rider more mobility in the saddle and allows him to handle the deep, hard stops and quick, 180° turns that cutting horses are famous for. The seat is deep so the rider can sit down in the middle of his horse and stay there, unlike saddles used for calf roping. A calf roper needs to get out of his saddle in a hurry, so his seat is shallow.

The horn of a cutting saddle is unique and no other saddle uses this type. Usually it is tall and narrow, making it easier to grasp during quick, hard maneuvers. The horn of a pleasure or reining saddle is generally little and short, really having no function at all. Roping horns are big and stout so the roper can dally his rope and hold a steer or calf.

The cutter wants to feel his horse underneath him and cutting saddles offer a close feel. By that I mean the saddle is constructed to keep the rider close to the horse. There is as little leather as possible between the rider's legs and the

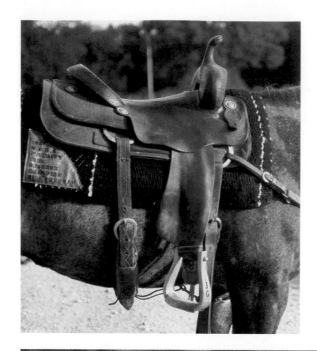

horse. Many other types of saddles have a heavy build-up between the rider's legs and the horse, with thick skirts and cinches positioned right where the rider's knees hit. Not only is this uncomfortable for the rider, but it also doesn't allow the rider to feel his horse.

Because we are all built differently, each of us is going to require a different size and style of saddle to be comfortable. I have my own personal preference. I like a saddle that is slightly raised toward the front end, however not as much as other saddles might be. The little bit of a rise gives me a pocket to sit in. I don't want my saddle to be real wide in through the seat, either. I like the closeness and the feel of my saddle underneath me.

I do not like a saddle with too much of a rise, too flat a seat, or one with an excessively tall horn. For me, none of that is comfortable. But what is comfortable for me most likely won't work for a person who is a quite a bit larger or smaller. I recommend that you try out several saddles under actual cutting conditions and see which works best for you. You might seek the advice of a cutting horse trainer and let him watch you work. He can give you some good suggestions for the best type of saddle for you.

My saddles are all built on a 16-inch Buster Welch tree. A saddle with a larger tree feels sloppy to me. If you get a seat that is too long, then that bottom, or pocket in which you sit, will be moved forward when you grip the saddle horn. Many people with totally flat-seated saddles, or saddles that are too big, aren't secure in the saddle. A cutting horse often lowers his front end to control a cow. When he does, the rider in a big saddle ends up sitting too close to the swells, because gravity pulls him there. A saddle like this will have you constantly struggling to ride it, and will encourage a tendency to pull on the saddle horn.

To ensure that my saddles fit me well, I have them custom-made. There are many excellent saddlemakers in the cutting horse business, and I have saddles from many of them. The key to a good-fitting, custom-built saddle is the workmanship, and we're fortunate in the cutting industry to have a group of saddlemakers who can be proud of their work.

Not only does the saddle need to fit the individual, it also needs to fit the horse. Horses, just like their riders, come in different sizes. There are high-withered horses and mutton or low-withered horses. Some horses have short backs and some have long backs. There are stocky-built horses and thin, petite horses. Since horses are built differently, the same saddle will not fit them all.

If you have just one saddle, however, the main thing you need to do is make sure the saddle does not hurt your horse. You don't want the saddle to ride too far forward on his back where it might rub sores on him and interfere with his shoulder movement. The saddle's bars need to be wide enough to fit on the horse's back without pinching, especially over the withers. Any of these things can make the horse's back sore and when this happens, the horse will not want to work for you.

(previous pages) Using comfortable, properly fitted equipment enhances the success of any training program.

(opposite top left and top right) I have two favorite saddles. Both are Buster Welch tree, flat-bottom saddles. One saddle has flat bottom stirrups and the other has oxbow stirrups.

(opposite bottom) The horn on a cutting saddle is used as a balance point by the rider during competition.

STIRRUPS

I like a laminated wooden stirrup. The lamination provides strength, and therefore extra security. Besides, the wood is just more comfortable than steel. I have both oxbow and flat-bottom varieties.

SADDLE PADS OR BLANKETS

I like to use wool Navajo blankets because they are absorbent and wool is generally considered an excellent material to put against a horse's skin. It stays put and does not rub back and forth like a lot of synthetic materials do, thereby eliminating friction sores. Often I'll use some other sort of blanket to go between the Navajo and the saddle for extra padding. I save my nicer Navajo blankets for show.

HEADSTALL

When it comes to headstalls, I prefer the ear loop variety. I don't like a split-ear head stall. To me, the split ear never really fits a horse right. I definitely like a headstall that has some type of an ear placement to help keep the bit in place. Otherwise the headstall might slide down the horse's neck and cause his mouth to gape open.

I like a throatlatch on a headstall, because it helps keep the headstall in place. If you tie up your horse, the throatlatch will keep him from rubbing the headstall off. Also, if you have a stiff headstall and a snaffle bit, and you take hold of your horse, that headstall can flip off the top of his head. A lot of my snaffles have brow bands and throatlatches to keep the headstall from sliding back on the horse's neck or from falling off. This is just a safety precaution in the training pen.

Some horses look good in browband headstalls, especially if they have good heads. But this is personal preference. I do think you can get too gaudy looking, using some show horse bridles with too much silver trim. Or you can make your horse look like he is a ranch horse by using one of the buckaroo-style headstalls. The latter are often far too wide or thick for the small heads of most cutting horses. There is something to be said for simplicity.

BITS

My choice of bit usually depends on the horse I am riding and what training I am doing. My favorite bit is the snaffle. I use it to start colts as well as to correct older horses. I like a snaffle bit because it is only as severe as you make it. However, most bits fall in that category, since a bit is only as light as the hand controlling it. The snaffle allows me to move a horse around without scaring him. It gives me the ability to turn the horse to the right and left without creating fear from the bit.

The snaffle is more of a teaching aide than a disciplinary aide. I can get a horse's nose pulled around in an easy manner with the snaffle, yet I still have enough bit to use with authority if it is necessary to stop him.

The two types of snaffles I like best are the single twisted wire snaffle and the simple snaffle with a jointed mouth-

(opposite top) The snaffle is an excellent training device, because it has no contact with the curb chain and it has a broken bit instead of a rigid mouthpiece. The rider can be as demanding or as light as he desires.

(opposite bottom) Although there is not a lot of left-right control with a noseband, Bill will use one on a horse that carries its head high. A noseband makes it easier to pull the horse's head down.

piece and some copper inlay. I prefer the rings to be two and a half to three inches in diameter.

I like keeping a horse in a snaffle because there is no contact with the curb chain and it has a broken bit instead of a rigid mouthpiece, making it a good training device. Even though the snaffle can command serious respect from a horse, it can also be as light as the rider desires. The horse keeps his mind on training and consequently, he thinks more. You have to remember though, that all of this has as much to do with my hands—how light or how heavy I use them—as it does with the bit.

In the early stage of breaking a horse to ride, I like to use a combination of noseband and snaffle bit. But this depends on the individual horse. There are some horses that are not ready to carry a snaffle in the beginning. Such a horse may have a tender mouth and the snaffle would scare him at a point in his training where he is already apprehensive. If that is the case, I like to start him with the noseband and ride him more before proceeding to the snaffle. The type of noseband I use can be made out of rope or steel. It encircles a horse's nose, resting on the bridge of the nose, where it has an effect on the nerves located there. It's similar to a hackamore or bosal in design, but it's thinner and lighter.

There is not a lot of left-right control with a noseband, so I want to get the horse into a snaffle as soon as possible. Then I can establish control. Some people prefer hackamores or bosals because you have more control, but I've had good luck with nosebands in the early stages of training. I also use a sidepull from time to time. It, too, is a good piece of equipment for getting a young horse to give his nose. Sidepulls generally do not scare a horse or put as much pressure on nerves around the horse's nose as rawhide or leather hackamores do.

I usually put a noseband or sidepull on a horse that wants to carry his head high. Then it is easier to pull the head down. A snaffle might have the opposite effect. Pulling on it might make the horse's head go up even higher. However, on horses I'm not comfortable with, or horses that seem a little unmanageable (won't stop or turn well), I go directly to a snaffle bit for more control. There is a lot of side-to-side control with a snaffle bit. For a horse that acts up, one tug on a single rein definitely brings the horse's head around. He finds himself going in small circles and under the rider's control in a hurry.

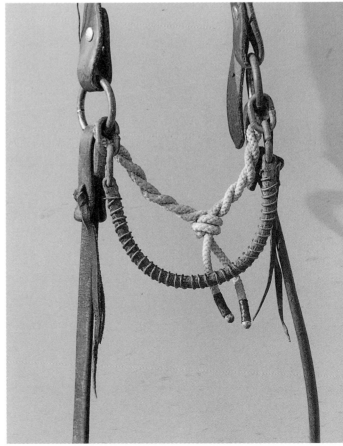

When a horse is comfortable with the training process, he will tell you he is ready to go to the snaffle. You will know this when he starts lugging or pushing on the noseband or running through it as if it didn't exist. Then it's time to go to the snaffle and regain control.

I am not a strong believer in the rope noseband. I don't feel I have much control of my horse when I am using it. It's fine to put on a horse if you want to really keep him soft. A rope nose band is a good tool for being really easy with your horse, but you are not going to teach him a lot in it.

I do use a Clapper bit, but not often. I use it with soured, older horses because it demands a lot of respect. I might use it on a horse that is a little temperamental, especially if you want more feel in the face, more response. It is a heavier, harsher bit and because of this, it must be used with a lot of thought so you don't create fear in the horse. You don't have to be severe when using it. Just the way it is made, the extra weight lets the horse know he needs to pay attention to you.

A good time to try the Clapper is when a stallion starts bowing up (resenting) at your teaching methods and gets that brazen look in his eye. He will change dramatically after being placed in the Clapper. That old "try me" look will be gone and in its place will be a look of respect. I will sometimes use it three or four times on a young horse and then go back to the snaffle. This method really matures the young horse.

Much of the way you use bits is a judgment call on your part. You have to use common sense when putting a bit in a horse's mouth. If you misuse a heavy bit, you can overdo a good thing. If you continue to hang tough with the heavier bit, you will soon wear out its usefulness. If you get the

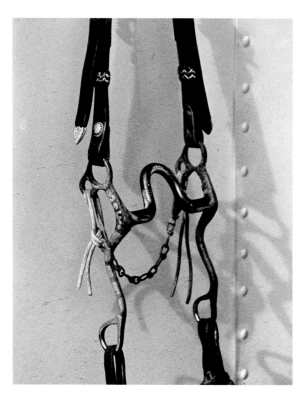

(above and right) Bill uses a Clapper bit with younger horses to help them mature. He will also use it to gain respect on older horses that are temperamental or sour.

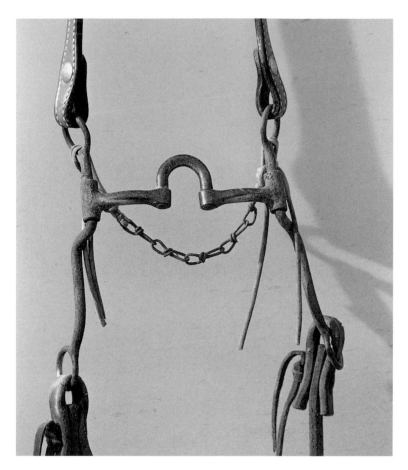

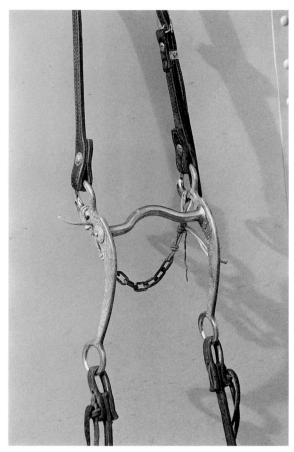

immediate response you want, especially for correctional purposes, then put the heavier bit back in the tack room and go on to something different.

When I show or tune up before a show, I like to use a bit that has some weight. One of my favorites is a correctional bit—a curb bit with relatively short shanks and hinged at the cheeks and mouthpiece. This is a hinged port bit; in other words, the port mouthpiece offers some tongue relief and hinges or swivels where the port is attached to the bars of the mouthpiece and where the mouthpiece attaches to the shanks. This bit has a lot of feel to it and I go with feel more than anything else. If I can have feel in a horse's face and have him respond positively to me, then that is the bit I want to use. You have to experiment to find out what your horse likes and respects. However, I have found this little correctional bit works well on most of my horses when I show them. It has a little bit of a bite and demands respect, yet it is not as rigid as a solid bit. To me it is a bit that combines the best of two worlds since it gives me mobility and bite. In other words, this bit offers the response or bite of a curb bit (a bit with shanks, which puts leverage on a horse's mouth). Yet the correctional bit also has the options of a snaffle (a bit without shanks or leverage, but great for lateral flexibility or right-left control).

I also like to use a Buster Welch bit, which has a low port. It's a mild bit and I use it often on younger horses. Bits with higher ports exert more pressure inside a horse's mouth and should be used with care. But I use them on

(above left)   One of Bill's favorite bits is a correctional bit since it has a little more weight and gives both mobility and bite. It is both a great training bit and a show bit.

(above right)   Each horse is an individual and requires different training devices. On some horses Bill will use a standard Buster Welch bit—a mild bit with a low port.

Even when Bill uses a curb bit on a horse, he stays in a training program and strives for control. The bit provides a lot of feel in the horse's face, permitting him to respond positively.

older horses who have become a little dull in the face, and are not as responsive to bit pressure as they used to be. Also, a bit with longer shanks exerts more leverage on the horse's jaw. A bit with a high port and long shanks will have a lot more authority in its effect on a horse than a bit with a low port and short shanks.

MARTINGALE

I use a martingale to keep the horse's head in proper position. I like to build my own martingales with a small (one-eighth inch) piece of slick nylon string, which has a little bit of give to it. This makes the martingale inexpensive and adjustable to the size of the horse I am working.

The type of martingale I use consists of a loop and three strings. The loop goes over the horse's head and neck and rests at the base of the neck. At a point, about midway on a horse's chest (where the center of a breast collar would be), one string attaches to the dee or ring in the center of the cinch. Two more strings extend toward the horse's chin. Each of these strings has a ring on the end through which the reins run, one on each side of the horse's neck.

With the horse standing relaxed, I adjust the martingale so the rings are set at the top of the neck. This prevents a horse from raising his head any higher than his withers. You do not want to adjust the rings any lower than neck level. They would be too short and would prohibit the horse from freely using his neck in a normal fashion. All you want is for the horse to meet resistance if he raises his head too high.

REINS

I prefer a heavy rein, approximately five-eighths of an inch thick, not only in training but also in the show pen. This type of rein gives me a little more stability. It doesn't flop and create a disturbance for the horse. Also, the heavier rein allows you to feel your horse and react accordingly.

SPURS

With respect to spurs, I prefer to use cloverleaf rowels in the training pen but I sometimes show my horse in dull rock grinders. Naturally it depends on the temperament of the horse. Almost all of my training is done in cloverleaf rowels because I can use them without scaring a horse or marking him up. I can use the cloverleaf variety more as a teaching tool, and not create fear in a horse.

I use regular rock grinders on some horses when I show because I can get more of an immediate response than I can with cloverleaf rowels. They give me a little extra touch or feel. If I am showing a tough-sided horse or a horse that is a little short consistently on one side or another, I might combine my spurs. I show in a cloverleaf on the horse's good side and a rock grinder on the side that needs a little extra encouragement.

PROTECTIVE BOOTS

Protective boots on horses' legs are insurance and I use them during practice as well as show. They help prevent a horse from banging and nicking himself, which in turn, reduces injuries and lay-up time. Nearly all the protective boots on the market are made of some shock-absorbing material and have VELCRO R fasteners. This makes them easy to get on and off in a hurry. Also, they come in sizes to fit almost any horse.

I use boots on both front and back legs. I use a longer boot behind than in front because the cannon bone on the front leg is shorter than the back cannon bone. The hind leg boot is long enough to cover the horse's fetlock. This relieves the stress and concussion of the stops and turns. You can also use longer boots on the horse's front legs if you prefer.

The martingale is an ideal piece of equipment for preventing a horse from raising his head.

145

16

A Winning Strategy

There is quite a bit more to showing a cutting horse than a two-and-a-half minute run. If you just ride into the arena without preparing yourself or your horse to show, then you are not working under the best show conditions.

Besides physical preparation, there are several things you can do before and during the show to help give your horse the best opportunity to use his skills. You have got to do your part to provide him with the chance to demonstrate his cutting ability or you won't be competitive.

MENTAL PREPARATION

Before it's my turn to show, I go over my game plan for my run. At that time, my mind is not on the horse, but on the cattle. I focus on the way I want to approach the herd, how deep I want to go, and how far I want to drive the cattle. Mentally, I go over those things that I have learned from studying the cattle. I try to find two to four cattle that I think will best suit the horse I am riding.

Getting yourself prepared mentally to cut is just as important as having your horse prepared physically, maybe more. Cutting is a mental sport every bit as much as it is a dynamic physical contest between horse and cow. And the horse, too, is using his mind to outsmart the cow as much as he is using his body to control the cow.

Maintaining a good mental attitude will help you develop winning runs. It is not hard to win the first time, but it is to win the second time, and to keep doing it is even harder. The first time you win is almost like luck. Naturally, you prepare, but you really don't have enough knowledge in the beginning to know the pitfalls, and therefore you don't

(above) Cee Fly Chick, a chestnut gelding by Fly Cee out of Jeannie's Chick and owned by Bill and Karen Freeman, won the 1985 NCHA Classic despite having only 50% vision in one eye due to an accident as a baby colt.

(previous pages) Studying cattle is an essential part of a competitor's performance.

worry about them. Then, when you really start learning the game, you put unneeded pressure on yourself as well as your horse to continue to win. This usually works against you rather than for you.

Cutting requires you to be mentally alert every second you perform. Instead of evaluating each situation, each horse, and each ride individually, we sometimes have a tendency to lump them all together. But that won't work. Once you have tasted what it is like to win, then you try to think back to what you did to win that first time. But that situation will not apply the next time you compete. It's doubtful you will cut the same type of cow and have it try your horse in the same manner as when you first won. In fact, it's doubtful that anything will be the same as when you won that first time. It's a whole new ball game every trip.

The main key is to adjust your program to the horse, not the horse to your program. If you do the former, you eventually will have a horse capable of winning. If you try to adjust the horse to your program, you may end up with confusion.

To be a winner, you have to think like a winner, you have to develop the thought that you are a winner in your mind. You have to have confidence in yourself and in your horses. I like to tell my students that they are down there to put on a performance. Even if he or she is an amateur, they have to sell that performance. The important thing about this sales job is that they have to sell it to themselves before they can sell it to the judge. You have got to believe in yourself before you can expect others to believe in you.

The arena is a big theatrical stage and you are putting on a performance. What you do with that opportunity is entirely up to your skills. If you are negative, it is going to show up in the way that you sit on your horse—shoulders humped a little and scared, instead of shoulders back and confident. It will show up in the way that you ride your horse—timidly or aggressively. And it will also show up in the way that you appear personally. If you don't radiate a positive attitude, then you are defeated before you go.

Horses are unique individuals. They can perceive through your body what you're thinking in your mind. You are telegraphing how you feel straight through your saddle. If you are nervous and scared, or if you are secure and confident, your body lets your horse know it.

If there is a problem you can't solve, then teach yourself to think about it in a more positive manner. Tell yourself, "I need to get help in learning how to do this," rather than saying, "I can't do this."

Another way to ensure positive thoughts is to associate with positive people. People have a tendency to behave like those they are around. So surround yourself with people who encourage one another, who say good things, and who are always looking for ways to improve.

Your mental work is not over when the buzzer sounds the end of your two-and-a-half minute run either. I never leave the cutting without analyzing my run. I play this run over in my mind no matter if I scored well or scored badly.

Peppy Lena San by Peppy San out of Cee Lena, a stallion that reminded Bill of Smart Little Lena, claimed the 1986 NCHA Derby Championship winning $95,832.00. Bill regards him as a complete horse, a winner, and an athlete with intelligence.

There is always something that can be learned. Even if I did well, I look for places where I could have helped my horse more, or where I might have hindered him.

If I scored badly, I try to figure out what went wrong in the run. It could be just the breaks of the game, such as slipping in the dirt or cutting a cow that ran over my horse. However, it could be something that I need to make myself aware of. Perhaps I did not prepare my horse correctly. I may have left him too fresh, or I may have ridden him too much and had him too tired.

If I can't figure it out, then I go to a fellow trainer and sincerely ask him for his opinion. This needs to be someone you can trust to tell you the truth. Someone who tells you that the judge just didn't score you fairly (when in reality you have some areas you do need to work on) will not help you do any better at the next cutting.

If I am not satisfied with the opinion of a fellow trainer, then I get someone to watch me work in a practice pen to see any mistakes. If none of this helps to explain my low score, then I forget it, and do not carry it on to the next cutting. That last cutting is history and if you cannot learn from it, then you forget it. Wondering about it and carrying it around with you would be a negative thought, and that is something you don't need. Never forget that every cutting is different and whatever you did at the last cutting to cause the low score may never happen again.

Cutting is a mental sport because there are few physical qualifications needed to actually ride and show a cutting horse. You don't need great strength. You don't have to be tall or short, and age is not a factor. To truly be at your best, though, you do have to think, respond, and be in tune with your horse. You have to be a part of your horse and make the horse a part of you. A good competitor and his cutting horse become an extension of one another.

To help me comprehend what my horse is going through, I have walked through a bunch of cattle to help me understand things better. It helps me visualize from a horse's perspective where I would stop a cow, and how I might react to a milling herd. I put myself in as many different situations as I can. Cutting a cow on foot helps you learn to read a cow.

Mental preparation is one of the biggest phases of cutting. It is not something that you do just at the show. In reality, it started a good year and a half ago when you first threw a leg over your horse, and it is something that you will need to continue to polish and hone as long as you enter a cutting arena.

STUDYING CATTLE

One of the first things I do at a show is study the cattle. I don't think it is absolutely imperative to study bunches that were worked prior to your turn, but it is advantageous. Usually cattle will follow a pattern. If the red-colored cattle are working good and all of the cattle for the show came from the same owner, then most likely the red cattle are going to be good in the next bunch. This applies to cattle that are worked on the same day. But if you don't work your horse until the next day, that might not be the case. The cattle might be totally different the following day.

When I study cattle, I try to learn several things about them. First, I get a feel for which side of the pen they are going toward when they are being moved around by the cutter. I watch to see if they try a cutter harder on one side than another. I analyze on which side of the pen the cows return faster after a group has been driven out. If the cattle return faster in one direction than another, then I cut away from that pressure point.

Every pen will have a side where cattle will hang up. It may be because of where they are fed. At the Will Rogers Coliseum in Fort Worth, they hang off to the east side of the pen. I also watch to see where in the pen the horses are struggling. Perhaps the ground is deeper on one side than the other.

I study cattle to know which ones have already been cut. They usually don't work as well as fresh cattle. I especially do not want to cut a cow that another horse lost because that cow has learned it can get back to the herd and might run over my horse doing it.

I watch to see what types of cattle are reacting best to the horses. I go through the run continuously in my mind while someone else is working. This helps me get in tune with the cattle and with what I want to do. If you make a mental note of all these things, you can adjust your run.

PRE-FUTURITY WORKS: WARMING UP FOR THE REAL THING

For futurity-aged horses (late 3-year-olds), preparation for major aged events may begin weeks before the competition. It is important that you do everything possible to prepare them for being away from home. This is called seasoning. A seasoned horse is one that is comfortable with new sights and sounds, and being away from the security of his own working pen and stall.

There are practice sessions, called pre-futurity works, that are held prior to some futurities. These simulated works place horses under show conditions without actual judging. They acclimate the horse to different arenas, lights, smells, and sounds. Because you are putting your horse in a strange environment, you need to pay attention to how he reacts to this environment. You can learn the best way to prepare him for the competition.

I usually find that I need to make some adjustments to a horse when I get him away from home. The pre-futurity work helps me find out how much I need to prepare him before showing. Under show conditions, I may need to lope him more to get him settled to work cattle, or I may not need to lope him as much. Every horse is different and you determine what he needs by trial and error. Often, I may not know whether the horse is prepared to work until I ride into the herd to cut a cow, so these pre-futurity works are a real asset. If he is too hyper, then I have not loped him enough. If he is too tired or disinterested, I may have loped him too much or maybe he needs to be "revved up" before we enter the herd.

In addition, there may be 40 to 60 other horses at the show. Your horse needs to get used to all the commotion made by both horses and people. At a show, he gets tied next to strange horses and loped among strange horses. The hauling, the different stalls, the close proximity with strange horses, the noise, the lights, and other distractions are all situations which he needs to learn to handle before going to the big show.

Each year we put on a pre-futurity practice at Abilene, Texas. We set up two pens in which to work. One pen is timed for five-minute works. Most of the cutters use this as a simulated big "Futurity" pen to see where they are at in showing their horse. A cutter can have two works per day per horse if necessary in this big pen. The other arena is not timed. We put a load of cattle in the pen, and everyone works their horse as they need to, respecting the needs of the other competitors there. This is the pen where you take your time and work your horse, rather than pretend you are working under actual show conditions.

A pre-futurity work can really enhance your training program. I have seen relatively green horses, who were unsure of themselves, gain confidence and put it all together during one of these pre-futurity works. They mature a lot when they have the opportunity to interact with other animals and people in new surroundings. Some horses will act like seasoned veterans before the works are over. A pre-futurity practice is an important extension of your training program and a wise investment for both you and your horse.

Learn to read cattle by studying their individual behavior and try to figure out what cattle have the best actions for the particular horse you are showing. Look for the obvious. You may not want to cut cattle with bad eyes or weepy eyes. As the cattle are being settled and the cutters in front of you are working, watch the reaction of the cattle to horses. There is no sure-fire method for recognizing a good cow versus a bad cow, other than the obvious fast or slow cow.

However, certain breeds have some common characteristics or tendencies, and I look for these when I cut one from the herd. In my opinion, Chianina, Semmental, Beefmaster, Limousin and

High Brow Hickory by Docs Hickory proved he was a true athlete by winning the Reserve Championship at the 1986 NCHA Futurity .

all exotic breeds tend to be dumb and quick. Native-bred cattle—Angus and Hereford (or black baldface), and Charolais—are usually your better cattle to cut. You are more likely to pick cattle from these breeds to fit your horse. They are tough, but often manageable, and they will let you pick up points if your horse can handle them. I do not like roan cattle. They are good for about four turns and then they run over you. The Charolais cow will usually try you pretty good. The black baldface cow is normally one of the better cows in the herd. In the past 10 years, the Hereford cow has become the cow not to cut. I like a Black Angus cow, especially a Brangus cow. They are usually quick. They come look for you and they like to work a horse. They can take you out of a cutting sometimes, but they can win one for you too.

Another ideal cow in my opinion is an extremely fresh Brahman. Such a cow has quickness, a lot of honor for your horse (respect), heads easily, and therefore, will let you show your horse.

Of course, there are exceptions to the rule, but I've seldom seen it. By learning about herd personalities, you will be more aware of what might happen during your run. Cattle will kind of follow suit. Usually the cattle for a specific day have all come from the same ranches. If the black cattle are good in one go-round, then they are usually decent in every bunch. Likewise, if they are not good in one bunch, chances are they will not be good all day. When all else fails, you have to step up and cut the cow that shapes best for you. Do not get tunnel vision. If you "feel" a cow seems good, then take a chance on her. If she will let you cut her in a good position, get her stopped, then that's the cow to cut.

It is just as important to know what you don't like as what you do like. I don't like a cow with a narrow head. Pig-eyed cattle or slant-eyed cattle are not going to be very good most of the time either. A cow that is not in good health will be fairly numb or phlegmatic and will not offer you a good opportunity to show your horse.

HERD HELP

When you're working your horses, and especially when you're competing at a show, your herd help can make or break you. According to NCHA rules, you can have four helpers—two herd holders and two turnback men.

The herd holders are positioned on each side of the herd. Their function is to hold the herd behind the cutter after the cutter has selected a cow. They can assist the cutter in cutting a cow. They can also assist you in seeing cattle. When you step back into the herd after quitting a cow, they might make a suggestion about a cow that acts really good. However, I prefer to do my own cutting. I only want my herd holders to help me locate a cow we discussed earlier. After that, their job is to hold the herd as I work the cow.

The other two riders, the turnback men, are positioned between the cutter and the judge. They stand about equal distance from each other, each controlling one half of the arena. Their job is to keep the flow of action going by turning the cow back toward the cutter as the cow tries to escape. Often, the cow tries to run past the turnback men and leave the scene. If the turnback men can force the cow back toward the cutter, the cutter can continue to work the cow. It doesn't look good to lose the cow, but it does happen.

It is to your advantage to communicate with your help about what you plan to cut. When you are last in the herd, this knowledge is even more crucial. Value the opinions of the four people that you have asked to help you. If you point out a cow that you want to cut and one of your help tells you the cow did not work well earlier, give his opinion serious consideration. If you trust him enough to help you with your run, then you should value his opinion about the cow. This is not to say that you have to take his opinion, just give it some consideration. Usually, though, the five of you putting your heads together will come up with better choices of cattle to cut than your making the decision alone. It is a team effort. Each of those helpers is trying to help the cutter win first.

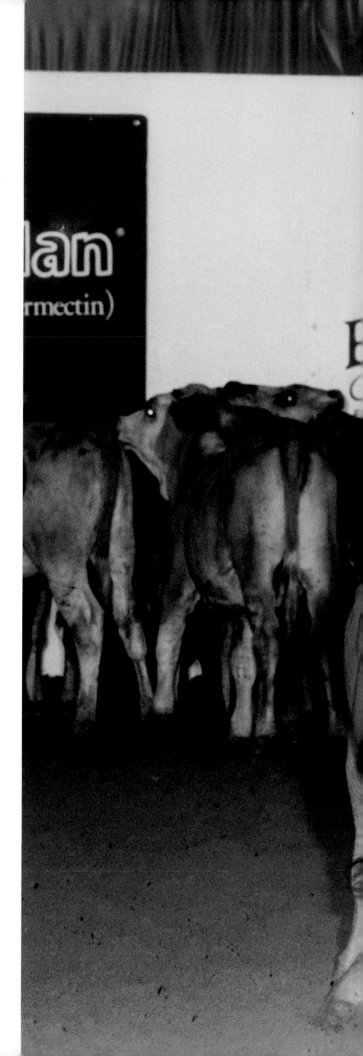

17

Show Time:
Cutting the Cow

After the months and often years spent training a horse to cut cattle, there comes a time to put it all together. The best way to find out how your training has worked is to put your horse to the test by competing in a cutting contest. Your work is not done yet, though. Showing a cutting horse is an art in itself. There's a lot to know and experience is always the best teacher.

ENTERING THE HERD - THE CUT

As you approach the herd, do not rush. Relax your back and use leg pressure to guide your horse to the right or left to assist the directions from your rein hand. When cutting a cow, hold the reins up, maintaining light contact with the bit. Later, when the cow is cut, your hand should go down on the horse's neck as required by NCHA rules. That is a signal that you have selected the cow you wish to work. Your hand must remain down during the entire time you work that cow. Otherwise, you will incur a one-point penalty for each time you move your hand. When you're finished working that cow, you can then raise your hands, return to the herd, and cut another cow.

Always look at the cattle, not your horse, because looking at the horse relays to a judge that you are unsure about him. That can lower your score.

If there is a cow on the back fence that you want to cut, push that cow to the inside or outside, wherever you want to move her, by using two or three other cattle to help move her. Try to drive that particular cow out with several other cattle to cushion your pushing her. It is essential to use a group of cattle to push out the cow that you may want to cut because you do not want to commit to a cow prematurely. She might tell you while driving her out that she is not good

(previous pages) Travelena was a horse that developed late in his career. He had a lot of charisma in front of a cow.

and you will need to change to another cow. Often, if a cow senses that you are trying to cut her, she will try to escape rather than move out with the other cattle. By using other cattle, you can put the desired cow where you want her so you can cut her.

Many cutters think that you systematically ride up in the cattle and push the herd out and cut a cow. But what if you get a crippled, or a blind, or a real lethargic cow in that group, and it interferes with the rest of the cattle? Or what if you end up with such a cow standing out there for you to cut? This is one of the reasons why I prefer to have a program when I enter the herd. During your study of the cattle, hopefully you have identified any with a problem.

17a—Bill holds his reins in his left hand and likes to enter the herd on the left side. The cattle will then curl to the right, making it easier for him to rein in and cut a cow on that side.

17b—If you ride straight toward a problem cow's head, you will have a better chance of moving her to the back wall and keeping her away from the group of cattle you drive out.

The best way to handle one of these problem cows is to ride straight to her as you enter the herd and push her to the back to get her out of the way or avoid her by cutting in the other direction. Hopefully, she will then stay on the back fence and you will not be bothered with her again. However, you can't forget about her when you make your second or third cut because there is always the possibility she has inched back to the front of the herd while you were working your cow.

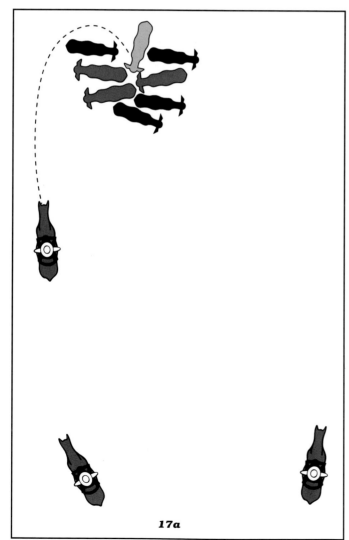

17a

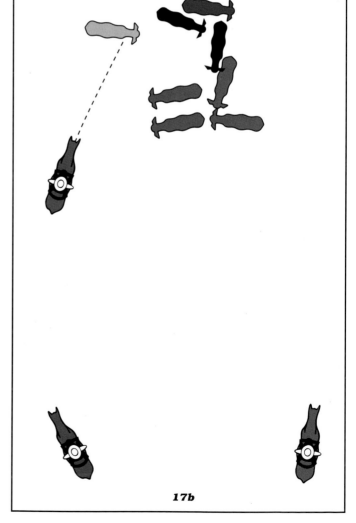

17b

I like to go up the left side of the pen because I hold the reins in my left hand. Then, when I move up through the cattle, they are going to curl to my right and it is easier to rein the horse into a cow on that side rather than pull that hand across my body. After they start curling to my right, I step over to the right to stop the flow, which will then make the cattle move to the left. When I do this, the cattle will start clearing away, but this gives me just a second longer to make my cut. Of course, a lot of this depends on my horse and which side of the pen I entered the cattle on. Sometimes location of the cattle in the herd tells me which side to enter.

Nearly everyone enters the cattle from the right-hand side. Cattle are not stupid. If they go around a horse quite a few times to the left, they are going to get faster each time they do this. If you draw a little bit later in the herd, by reversing that flow on them, you will gain a few extra seconds to step up into a cow.

When I bring out the herd to cut a cow, I always look at all of my cattle to get a good overall picture of what they're like. Usually, I study the front of the herd because one of those cows is probably the one I want to cut. However, I do pay attention to all that happens around me. If another cow hits the cow that I had my eye on and runs her off, I need to have another cow in mind to cut. In other words, you can't have "tunnel vision" about one cow when you are driving a group of cattle out to cut. You need to read more than just one cow.

Before I commit to a cow, I pay attention to the way the cow reacts to me or to the surroundings. If she is banging into other cattle, I disregard her because she is telling me that she is not very smart. I watch for any move she makes that tells me she is not going to be good, like throwing her head up or making sudden moves. If she does these things in the herd, she will be worse when she is separated.

Sometimes while stepping up through the cattle with the cow you want to cut, but are obviously not committed to, she may do a little something that tells you to beware. This may be flicking an ear back at you, or the way she twitches her tail or rolls her eyes. Go with your first instinct. Disregard this cow and cut another, one that feels better or one that you have discussed. This is another reason why you should know the cattle. As you are stepping up through the herd, use your intelligence, use your feel.

Learning to read cattle is a very important step in cutting. You can have a scorpion of a horse, but if you cannot get a good cow to show him on, no one will ever know his ability.

So many people believe they don't have much time to make a cut and so they hurry. Neither do they have any idea which cow to cut. Between having no program and rushing, they get themselves ambushed and run over.

If you take a little more time to prepare the cut and move the herd around, push them hard enough, and then back away from them once or twice; you can get a feel for how they are reacting to you. Then you'll get a good cut most of the time.

Smart Little Senor, 1988 NCHA Futurity. Out of Smart Little Lena's second colt crop to go to the Futurity, Smart Little Senor was Freeman's third Futurity champion.

Many cutters do their homework well and then come up through the herd of cattle with one cow in mind to cut. They have a tendency to disregard anything else going on and get tunnel vision on that cow. That is human nature, but it is not the best thing to do. You always need a back-up plan.

While you are cutting the cow, through its actions it says to you, "I am not a good cow," then you must be flexible enough to have other options. If you have a feel for all the different cattle in your bunch, then you have something you can fall back on. You have to develop this ability to adjust while you are in the herd. Your concentration level must be high and focused. Still, you must be flexible enough to make an immediate decision to leave "Plan A" should the first cow signal to you she is not good, and go to "Plan B."

To have a good cut, you want to set up a cow before she even knows that she is being set up. This starts when you ride into the herd. You can maneuver her around using several other cattle between you and her. You calculate where she is going, and if that is not appropriate, you stop her by angling your horse in that direction. While you work the herd, you also evaluate how much the cow is going to let you push her. Again, if you don't feel good about her reaction, then you abandon her and take up "Plan B."

Use your legs in the process of making a cut. Anybody you see who has his rein hand really elevated is not only panicking, but also has forgotten that he can use his legs. He is trying to accelerate with his hand; but remember, you give direction with your hand and accelerate and motivate a horse with your legs and feet. The NCHA rule book states that credit will be given for actually working the herd. If you do it right, you will always receive credit.

If the cow you picked signaled that she was not a good cow and your next plan did not work out either, then cut for position or shape. Cutting for position or shape means that you cut the cow that wants you to cut her or will let you cut her. Most of the time, that cow is standing dead center of the pen. This is usually not the cow you selected in the first place, but because of the circumstances, it will have to do. As I stated earlier, a lot of competitors cut for position all of the time. I prefer to have a little more knowledge about my cow if at all possible.

I prefer to cut a cow that has stopped. However, I want to be moving to that cow, or at least have my horse faced up to her, his eyes on the cow when the cutting starts. When my hand goes down, I am going to press that horse toward the cow to get the run started. I want to control that first initial move. The danger is being dead still and waiting for your help to start a cow. If you just sit and wait for the cow to move, you don't know if your horse has hold of the cow or which direction it is going to go.

However, when you start the cow yourself, you can also dictate which direction the cow will move. This is a simple little technique in which you place your horse just off center. Then move at an angle toward the cow so she moves in the direction you want her to go. This works about 80 percent of the time. It is a lot safer to move to the cow and have total control. If you wait, then the cow has control.

In my clinics, I make people cut cattle on foot. It is very interesting how they usually can do it correctly on foot, but so often they do not relate to this scenario when horseback. Cutting is very much a mental game and you should always be thinking. Most of the people who cut a cow on foot always stay facing the cow. Yet often they will turn sideways or parallel to the cow when they to try to cut a cow horseback.

FIRST IN THE HERD

For the rider who draws up first, the cattle are fresh and have not experienced a horse in their midst. The first time a horse enters the herd, the cows will follow each other to get away from the horse. I don't want to bring that many cows out when I go in to cut that first cow. So I try to drive out only a few, but it's easy to end up with half of them anyway.

I want to get a real good push on the group of cattle. I want to drive them farther out than I normally would if I worked later in the bunch. Doing this allows plenty of room to work the cow I cut without disturbing the herd.

Since I am the first cutter, the herd won't be quite as compact (herd-bound) behind me. They will have more of a tendency to run out. Therefore, I want to make sure I drive my cattle out and get far enough away from them so I won't get charged penalty points for disturbing the herd or picking up cattle.

LAST IN THE HERD

When you draw last in the herd, it is imperative that you study the cattle and know what has been worked, what has not been worked, and what your best options are. You want to watch for cattle that acted good when they were worked the first time because if you can't find any other good cattle, rerun cattle might work good a second time.

There is no set rule as to which cow is going to work best. Typically, a "fresh" cow, one that has not been worked, would be better to cut than a cow that has already been worked. However, working last in the herd may or may not afford you any fresh cattle. A fresh cow that is left may have been jostled around so much every time someone cut a cow, that she might be angry and not desirable to cut. She might want to run over your horse or just go numb and not move. In such a situation, a rerun cow that worked well previously might be a wiser choice than the fresh cow. This is another reason why you must read your cattle and know from their body language which might work for you and which against.

If I know the cattle are bad and won't let me push them out, then I penetrate the herd dead center so that one side will start to come around me. Coming straight into the herd, rather than from the side, will cause one side of the cattle to come around. When they start going around me, I can back up or enter the herd deeper to push more cattle; or I can even turn and attach myself to the group of cattle moving around me. Since I am in the middle of the cattle, by turning in the same direction they are going, I encourage the bunch of cattle that is standing still to move toward the cattle coming around me, thus causing a collision point. At that collision point, I then start my horse up through the herd. One of two things will happen. The cattle will either push each other or hesitate for a moment, and that is all I need to come up through them and get a cow cut. Usually in this situation, I'll cut for shape, stepping to the cattle aggressively.

DYING IN THE HERD

"Dying in the herd" is a phrase which means that you were in the herd trying to cut a cow when the buzzer sounded, ending your run. Years ago, it was considered bad for your run if you died in the herd. Today, it's not always something that works against you. How you and your horse have performed in the previous two and a half minutes is the deciding factor on how dying in the herd affects your score. If you have had enough working time during your run, then dying in the herd is just a part of the process of cutting a cow. As long as you make it clear that you are trying to get another cow cut, then you are doing your job.

However, dying in the herd will affect your score if you have not spent much of your two and a half minutes working a cow, or if you are not demonstrating that you are trying to cut another cow before the buzzer. For example, if you have already fulfilled your obligation for a deep cut (See Chapter 18 "Playing by the Rules") which you should have by this time in your run, then riding slowly to the back wall and moving the entire herd out in the same slow manner (which is another deep cut) does not demonstrate to a judge that you really desire to get another cow out to work for a few seconds before the buzzer sounds.

At the same time, I am not a strong believer in peeling a cow off the edge of a herd just for the sake of getting one cut before the buzzer sounds. It is a dangerous situation, one in which you will always be in a hurry, so I prefer not to do it. It's easy to make mistakes that way. You are exposing yourself to a penalty point in a situation like this. If the cow breaks and runs and you do not have your horse focused on him, then you will need to rein him to help him get started. You'll cost yourself a penalty point for reining your horse. (For more on penalties, see Chapter 18 "Playing by the Rules.")

For these reasons, I prefer not to peel cattle. It is better to do your herd work correctly. Even though you may feel that you have not gotten enough done during your run, it is still better to just stay on that second cow rather than risk adding more penalty points. If you have time to methodically cut another cow, then that is what you need to do. But if your limited time is going to force you to peel one off, for me it has always worked better to stay with my second cow.

BLIND CATTLE

If you have ever cut a blind cow, you'll realize why you need to study the cattle and communicate with your herd holders. You can usually locate these cattle by their actions while you are studying the cattle before you cut.

This is one of those areas in which your herd holders can really help you. If all of you are aware of a cow that is blind, then you can work together to try to prevent that cow from being out in the group from which you must cut.

I always discuss a blind cow with my help. I have them try to move that cow to the back of the herd before my time starts. If they cannot accomplish that, then when I ride down there to cut my first cow, I try to do it. If possible, I might approach the cow straight on and try to drive her to the back of the herd. Or, if she is on the right-hand side of the herd, I might approach the herd on the left-hand side in an attempt to keep her from coming with the cattle that I will be driving out.

To get a good performance by your cutting horse requires more than just riding him into the arena. There are many factors, especially when working with cattle, that can change your performance from average to successful.

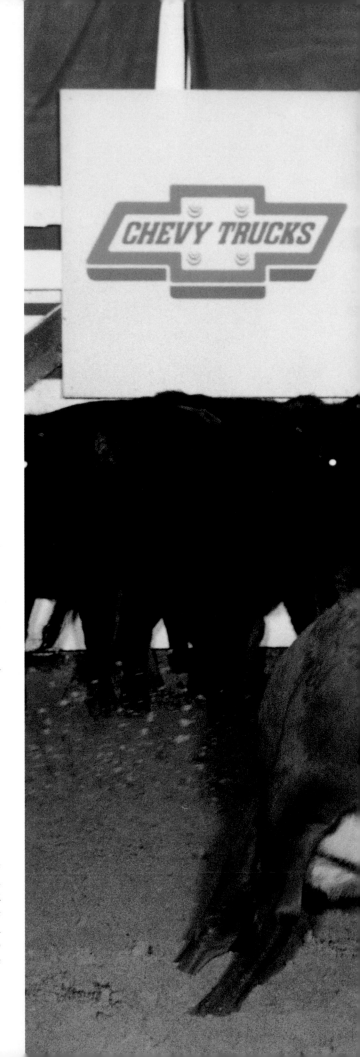

18

Playing by
the Rules

The point system used to determine your cutting score in most of the shows in which you will compete is based on the rules established by the National Cutting Horse Association. A Rule Book, as well as a Case Study Book, is available from the National Cutting Horse Association in Fort Worth, Texas.

To really be competitive in the cutting arena, an exhibitor needs to seriously study these rules and understand their interpretation. Twenty one rules, several with subtopics, determine how well you will be scored after you perform. Below I have reprinted several of the rules, with the permission of the National Cutting Horse Association, to assist you in areas which may cause penalty points in your cutting performance.

> *1.) Each horse is required to enter the herd sufficiently deep enough to show his ability to make a cut. One such deep cut will satisfy this rule. Failure to satisfy this requirement will result in a three (3) point penalty.*
> *a.) a horse will be given credit for his ability to enter the herd quietly with very little disturbance to the herd or to the one brought out.*

Notice in this first rule that it is not the number of cattle driven out that makes a difference, but the route that you take. There is no specific number of cattle to satisfy that rule. The number of cattle in a bunch varies with the number of cutters participating in the bunch. That magical number is in the judge's mind. The main point here is to go deep, to satisfactorily step behind a number of cattle before you start stepping up through them. You do this slowly,

(previous pages)   A strong horse and a big mover, Spurs and Roses is by Freckles Playboy and out of Kimberlena—a mare named after Freeman's daughter.

quietly, and smoothly with the purpose of singling one cow from the rest of herd, and cutting her dead still in middle of the pen. Once this is accomplished, you will then slowly step up to the cow as your hand goes down toward the horse's neck. Initiating the action this way makes sure your horse has hold of the cow. If you go deep into the herd, enter it quietly, bring a cow out quietly, and with little disturbance to the herd, you will receive credit for your cut.

4. Credit will be given for setting up a cow and holding it in a working position as near the center of the arena as possible.

Your objective with this rule is to cut the cow in the middle of the pen and to keep her there as much as possible while you are working her. Once again, the procedure discussed in rule #1 will help you cut the cow in the middle of the pen. You must continually think while cutting and try to anticipate actions before they happen. As you start up through the middle of your cattle, you must consider the route the cattle are taking at that precise moment. If the cattle are not going in the direction that you desire, then you stop the flow of the cattle by angling your horse slowly to head them off from that direction and push them back.

After you have made a cut in the center of the pen, keeping the cow there requires a lot of skill from you and your horse as a team. Hopefully you have chosen a good cow that wants to honor your horse and work with him. Now is when all of the training sessions you gave your horse to teach him to read a cow, and learn to draw a cow, will pay off. These two abilities that your horse should have by now help to keep the cow trapped in the middle of the pen. Likewise, your assistance in riding him as hard as needed, sitting easy when necessary, and encouraging him with leg pressure will guide him and help build his confidence that he can hold that cow in the middle of the pen. With trial and error, you, too, will learn to anticipate the actions of a cow, thus "read the cow" like your horse does and be prepared for action.

5. If the cutting horse or his rider creates distur- bance at any time throughout his working period, he will be penalized:
a. Any noise directed by the contestant toward the cattle will be penalized one (1) point.
b. Each time a horse runs into the herd, scatters the herd while working or picks up cattle through fault of the horse, he will be penalized three (3) points.
c. The judge shall stop any work because of training or abuse of his horse by the contestant or disturbance of the cattle. Any contestant failing to stop immediately will be penalized $500 payable to NCHA prior to entry in any other NCHA approved event.

If you are penalized for subtopic b. during a run, then, as a competitor, there are several things that you need to consider. Analyze the variables and decide what caused your horse to run through the herd or to pick up a cow. Did cow pressure cause this to happen? Did you stay too long on a cow? Did your horse cause it? If your horse created this problem by falling back too deeply while working the cow, then you need to get a little more control over him in the practice pen. The chapter on Control discusses this. Getting control will release that cow fear, which is causing him to fall back into the herd. He wants to get away from the cow.

After you have gained control in the practice pen, you can ride him up into that cow instead of having him fall away from the cow. Stepping him up keeps him aggressive and hooked to a cow, directly opposite of falling back, which is his way of trying to release the pressure of the cow.

6. A horse will be penalized three (3) points each time the back fence actually stops or turns the animal being worked within one step (3 feet) of the fence; the back fence to be agreed on and designated by the judge or judges before the contest starts; meaning the actual fence only, no imaginary line from point to point to be considered. If any of the contestants voice an objection before the contest starts, the judge or judges shall take a vote of the contestants, and a "back fence" acceptable to the majority shall be designated and used.

In competition, the back fence is the area in which the herd is contained. This area is agreed upon before the cutting starts and a marker is placed on each side of the arena. If the horse or rider enter the area, then a three-point penalty per judge is assessed.

There are two major reasons for back-fencing a cow. The first reason is poor judgment in your selection of a cow to work. Sometimes, a cow will "lie" to you, however. That means it gives you all the signals that it will be a good cow to work and then it will not honor your horse. Instead, it will try to run over you, and if your horse is able to hold it, often he receives a back-fence penalty during his efforts. This is just one of the breaks of the game and most often the case when back-fencing happens.

If, however, you select poor cows time and again, you need to reconsider how you are selecting your cattle. If you are studying the cattle prior to cutting and continuously selecting bad cattle, then get a more experienced trainer to help you learn these ropes.

Another reason for back-fencing can sometimes be rider error. It is essential that you learn to block out everything else while you are cutting, so that your timing will be perfect. Should you hesitate just a split second before riding your horse into a cow, then the cow will grasp the advantage, and push your horse back, thus causing a back fence.

BILL FREEMAN'S WINNING RECORD

— 1976 NCHA Reserve World Champion —
Jay Freckles

— 1976 NCHA Futurity Reserve Champion —
Doc's Becky

— 1979 NCHA Futurity Champion —
Docs Diablo

— 1980 NCHA Classic Champion —
Doc A Chex

— 1982 NCHA Futurity Champion —
Smart Little Lena

— 1983 NCHA Superstakes Champion —
Smart Little Lena

— 1983 NCHA Derby Champion —
Smart Little Lena

— 1984 Masters Champion —
Smart Little Lena

— 1985 NCHA Classic Champion —
Cee Fly Chick

— 1986 NCHA Derby Champion —
Peppy Lena San

— 1986 NCHA Futurity Reserve Champion —
High Brow Hickory

— 1988 NCHA Futurity Champion —
Smart Little Senor

— 1989 NCHA Futurity Reserve Champion —
Commandicate

— 1990 Breeders Cup Champion —
Commandicate

Commandicate, 1989 NCHA Futurity Reserve Champion. Probably the strongest horse Bill ever rode. Commandicate is by Smart Little Lena and out of a Mr Linton mare.

8. While working, a horse will be penalized one (1) point each time the reins are used to control or direct the horse, regardless of whether the reins are held high or low. A one point penalty shall also be charged whenever a horse is visibly cued in any manner. If the reins are tight enough that the bits are bumped at any time, he shall be penalized one point each time even if the hand of the rider does not move.

Sometimes you are unaware that you are moving your hand; however, that is not going to keep you from getting a penalty. Often the positioning of your body while you are riding can cause you to move your hand. This is one reason to work with a good professional because he or she will be honest and tell you these things before you get to the show and get penalized.

Use video tapes of your runs to learn why you are being penalized. Analyze these tapes. Watch them over and over. They do not stress good points and they accent the mistakes, so you can learn a lot from them. Get professional help and study the tapes until you figure out what created the movement.

Perhaps you are uncomfortable with your horse and, therefore, subconsciously helping him. Perhaps you are riding him poorly instead of flowing with the horse's movements. If you are tightening up, this will create a jerk so that your hand is going to move. Or perhaps your mind is just playing games with you. Remember, cutting really is a mental sport.

9. If a horse lets an animal that he is working get back in the herd, he will be penalized five (5) points.

Many things can cause this major problem. It could be pilot error from staying on a cow too long. It could be poor cow selection. It could just be bad luck. Your horse could be reading a cow incorrectly. Maybe he is not focused on a cow as he should be and is creating his own problems. Maybe it's just a bad day; maybe it's nobody's fault.

There are many reasons for this problem. If you spend too much time analyzing it, you will be dwelling on the negative, and you shouldn't do that. If you lose a cow and analyze the run and find no one is at fault, then disregard it and go on. If you figure out what caused it, then you go home and fix it.

For example, if it is lack of concentration and focus, you need to continually bring your horse back to the cow and build that concentration. If your horse is continually losing a cow, yet he is extremely athletic, he is probably making mistakes and overextending himself. You can correct this in the practice pen by drawing him back inside the cow and keeping him working tight with the cow.

If you are riding a horse that doesn't have enough athletic ability to overcome losing a cow even though he is trying his heart out, then that's the breaks. It is time to say my horse just can't do this.

Losing a cow is a chance that you take every time you ride to the herd. The main point is that you fix the problem if it is possible. Certainly don't dwell on it, because this will create an attitude of defeat.

10. If a rider changes cattle after visibly committing to a specific cow, a five (5) point penalty will be assessed.

The main thing you do to keep from switching cattle is to be decisive in what you want to cut. Being as deliberate as you can be when you start to cut your cow is the best remedy for removing doubt from a judge's mind.

If your horse picks a wrong cow or if the horse is trying to take every cow in the pen, then you need to go back to homework. Practice repetition in cutting: step up to the cattle, back away, move right or left, then back away. Continue until you feel comfortable with your horse's performance.

Another reason your horse may be doing this is because he is fresh. You solve this problem by loping him more prior to showing. This helps control his adrenalin before going to the herd. Also trotting and stopping your horse frequently help to gain that necessary respect you need before riding to the herd. These are things that you only find out under show conditions, so don't be surprised when the horse you have at home is quite different the first couple of times you take him to a show.

13. A contestant may quit an animal when it is obviously stopped, obviously turned away, or obviously behind the turnback horses and the turnback horses are behind the time line. A penalty of three (3) points must be charged if the animal is quit under any other circumstances.

This is called a "hot quit" and this penalty is always a rider error. To avoid this penalty, be sure of the direction of the cow or that the cow is completely stopped before you quit working. Otherwise, you may react to your horse, that is telling you by his actions that it is time to quit. This can definitely create a panicky feeling and cause you to quit the cow at an inappropriate time. To be safe, make sure the cow turned tail and moved away from you before you quit. In other words, make sure you are looking at his back end when you quit. Although you did this in response to your horse, you are still the one in control and you must make sure the correct opportunity is there before you quit the cow. If you put yourself in the position to get called for a hot quit, then most of the time you deserve the hot quit penalty. This all goes back to being in control of your own actions and then being decisive about them.

14. If a horse quits a cow, a penalty of five (5) points will be assessed.

Usually when you receive this penalty it is the horse's fault; but it, too, can be rider error. You can put so much pressure on your horse that he will just quit cutting out of frustration. If this is what happens, then you need to change your tactics for training.

If your horse is running off instead of staying hooked and working the cow, you have major troubles. The first thing you do is take him back to the practice pen and remain there until you feel that you have him secured at home. The horse is running off for a reason, and you need to search for that reason. Maybe he cannot handle the intensity of your program. Maybe he is hurting and doesn't want to turn, and runs off so he won't have to turn. Maybe he just doesn't want to be a cutting horse.

Running off is the most difficult problem to correct. If your horse is not hurting, then the first thing to do in trying to solve this problem is to slow everything about your training program down, way down. You have got to build your horse's confidence back up before you can put any pressure on him in the cutting arena, and you do this by slowing down to a snail's pace. Accept that this is going to be a long, slow process because to rush this step will only set you back further.

After you believe that the horse has regained some confidence, then go back to working on control. (See Chapter Three on "Control.") Let him know that the cow is not going to hurt him. At the same time, continue to build him up. Make him think he is superman by continually installing confidence in him. Remember that this is done at a slow pace. Step into the cow saying to your horse, "There she is, but she won't hurt you." When he finally begins to understand this, cutting will once again be easy and fun because you took away the pressure.

> **15. If a horse clears the herd with two or more cattle and fails to separate a single animal before quitting, a five (5) point penalty will be charged. There is no penalty if time expires.**

When two cows get paired, it is sometimes a comedy of errors. Since you have four other people trying to help you, everybody seems to get in everybody else's way in an attempt to solve this problem.

First and foremost, you cannot quit and go back into the herd without a five-point penalty. You have to stick it out, you have to separate the two cows and work one of them unless the whistle blows.

The first thing you should do is try to get aggressive and step in between them, separating them yourself rather than waiting for your help to do so. This is the best thing to do. If this doesn't get immediate results, then you slow down and back away and wait for your opportunity to step up when they separate themselves. Sometimes the more pressure that you place on the two, the more they bang into each other. If you back off, you are saying to them, "Here is the herd," and one of them will usually try to return to it.

Working within the parameters of the rules is a must in a cutting contest. Therefore, as a competitor, you need to know what techniques can give you credit and why other techniques can cause you penalties. Make certain that you have the correct interpretation of the cutting rules since one misunderstanding might cost you a cutting. If you have some questions, work with a professional for a hands-on experience or call the NCHA office for a thorough explanation of the rules.

"HE'S BEAUTIFUL INSIDE AND OUT.
HE'S ONE IN A MILLION."

19

The Saga of Smart Little Lena

Although Bill Freeman had ridden several good horses to championships, it wasn't until the early eighties that his name became synonymous with one particular horse, Smart Little Lena. The life of the stallion who excited the cutting horse industry by winning the first Triple Crown of the National Cutting Horse Association is like a fairy tale, a story of an ugly duckling who unfolds into a beautiful swan.

Smart Little Lena, a July 19, 1979, foal was not only a late foal by performance horse standards, but also definitely an ugly duckling at birth. His scrawny, homely body defied any dreams of greatness of his owners, Hanes and Antoinette Chatham. However, from the first time the meager little colt opened his eyes, he exhibited an exceptional personality, a unique disposition that separated him from the other weanlings.

"He was just different," remembered Antoinette. "He didn't have much to do with the other foals. In fact, the others picked on him, so he stayed by himself. But there was just an aura about him; you could see even as a little guy that he had so much talent."

"He was so ugly though," added Hanes. "Someone suggested we name him 'the ugly Doc-ling'".

It was as if Smart Little Lena knew he was destined to be a cutting horse. As a young colt, he displayed his inherited characteristics by watching butterflies. While other colts quietly grazed with heads to the ground, Smart Little Lena intuitively picked out butterfly after butterfly flitting among the wildflowers and stalked them. It became a ritual that everyone wanted to watch, not only because a colt was stalking a butterfly, but because of the moves he made. To those with cutting horse savvy, the way he stalked foretold his future. He flowed. His long legs floated across the

(above) Hanes Chatham and Bill knew they had a winner in Smart Little Lena long before the stallion demonstrated his ability at the 1982 NCHA Futurity. He radiated a unique, indescribable charisma which spelled success.

(previous pages) Smart Little Lena, 1982 NCHA Futurity Champion.

pasture almost in sync with the butterfly's wings. It was a hypnotic, mesmerizing movement resembling the beauty of a working cutting horse.

Although he felt he had an exceptional horse, Chatham consigned the stallion to the NCHA Futurity Sale as he did many of his young horses. However, after breaking and riding the colt, he called cutting horse trainer and friend, Bill Freeman.

"Hanes broke him in August of his 2-year-old year when he was 25 months old. When he called me in October about training him, he told me he had a colt with a lot of movement, an electric kind of horse that was real cowy. He also admitted the colt was sure green and a sure-enough little horse," grinned Bill, who had his doubts at that time about a green, little horse. However, he agreed to give Smart Little Lena a try.

"I was so impressed after just a couple of rides that I called Hanes and asked him what he wanted for the colt. He told me he would only sell half of him so we decided to form a venture. I would buy half of the horse and then we would sell 20 shares in him for $5,000 each."

The two felt they had several benefits in the stallion. He had a blue-blooded pedigree. He was sired by Doc O'Lena, an NCHA Futurity winner and sire of an NCHA Futurity winner, Lenaette, in 1975. He was out of Smart Peppy, an own daughter of Peppy San, that was also a full sister to one of the greatest cutting horses of all time, Royal Santana. The latter has been a major player in the cutting horse arena for two decades and was twice an NCHA World Champion in the non-pro division. Because of these impressive bloodlines, the newly formed partnership saw their horse as a well-bred stallion prospect. Add the outstanding cutting ability that Freeman and Chatham had witnessed, and the two partners felt sure others would want a share in their future money-maker.

But those who came looking did not see green bills. Instead, they saw a runt of a horse, only 13.3 hands tall, that had yet to blossom with beauty or size. When the two men told potential shareholders that Smart Little Lena was born late and started late, but, they promised, he was "coming on strong," their speech often fell on deaf ears.

"We begged, borrowed, tried everything to get people to buy into him," remembered Freeman.

Proving himself to share owners was not the only major obstacle that Smart Little Lena overcame in his 3-year-old year. He endured problems of sickness and injury that only proved his exceptional ability to beat the odds.

"That fall I took my futurity colts to Terry Riddle's to get them away from home," said Freeman. "I got there late one evening and Terry's help had already put feed in the stalls. The next morning when my help brought my horses, Shoo Fly Cee and Smart Little Lena, to the indoor arena, Shoo Fly Cee acted colicky. A vet came, but nothing he did relieved the pain, so at his suggestion, we sent the horse to Oklahoma State University in Stillwater. By the time they arrived in Stillwater, he was dead."

A quick autopsy showed that Shoo Fly Cee had died from blister beetle poisoning from the alfalfa hay they had been fed the night before. There was immediate concern for Smart Little Lena; at that time, he was showing no ill side effects. Freeman felt relieved when he found Smart Little Lena's hay still in the hay rack, since it, too, was full of blister beetles. It appeared that the stallion, accustomed to grass hay rather than alfalfa, had not eaten it.

But Smart Little Lena was not to slide by the incident without a battle of his own. Although he had not eaten all the hay, he must have taken a bite laced with a small amount of cantharidin. This is a poisonous substance secreted by the beetles that is toxic to the equine kidney and digestive tract. Not liking the taste, he ate no more and thus saved his own life.

"A short time later, Little Lena began experiencing some discomfort," remembered Freeman, "and before long he was in terrible pain with severe cramping and showing signs of shock. The vet was right there and worked with him all night

After winning the 1983 NCHA Derby, Smart Little Lena became a Triple Crown Winner.

Every year after Smart Little Lena returns from his months at the breeding farm, Bill saddles the stallion and they head for the cutting pen—a tradition at the Freeman Ranch.

long, calling every vet who had ever battled blister beetles and trying every remedy. It was scary for all of us. But about daybreak the next morning he started coming out of it."

The blister bugs were isolated to one bale of hay, so no other horses were affected. Smart Little Lena quickly rallied from his crisis and after 10 days of rest, was back in the cutting pen again. Besides the bout with blister beetles, the stallion also developed stifle problems as a 3-year-old.

"We flew Gary Kaufman, an outstanding vet from Arizona, to Wichita Falls to do the surgery. At that time, Terry had the only laser around, so after surgery we sent Terry up there where they used the laser machine on Smart Little Lena twice a day and exercised him daily. Once again he rapidly recovered and I was back working him on cattle in two weeks."

Even though Smart Little Lena demonstrated an astounding ability to overcome obstacles, even though he had blue-blood genes, and even though Freeman and Chatham offered persuasive stories about the stallion's potential to win big bucks, they still had not completely sold out of syndicate shares by NCHA Futurity time. For the 17 new owners who had shown faith, Smart Little Lena did not let them down. He grabbed everyone else's attention also by winning the first two go-rounds and finished second in the semi-finals of the Futurity.

"I was a little apprehensive about my draw in the Futurity finals," Bill said. "I was last in the first group, but Smart Little Lena could handle just about anything I could get him into. I knew that because I had gotten him into some bad places! That night I watched the cattle to know what not to cut; other than that, I cut just for position and shape."

Several high scores were already recorded. The leader at the time the pair rode to the herd was Brinks Leo Hickory with a score of 222. After Smart Little Lena finished his run, his nonstop, smooth action earned him a score of 225. The last horse to work that evening, Sugs Gay Lady, was his closest threat, scoring 223 with her run. For his victory, Smart Little Lena earned the Futurity crown and earnings of $267,084.56, his first of many checks.

After the NCHA Futurity, Smart Little Lena was a major topic of conversation in cutting horse barns. Because of all the widespread interest in the stallion, the newly formed syndication decided to sell an additional 10 shares, but raised the price to $25,000 per share. Although many people showed interest, no one wrote a check until once again Smart Little Lena enticed them with his phenomenal ability.

"The following January at the Atlantic Coast Futurity, he marked a 225 in the first go-round, the highest score ever recorded at that show. He then returned to win the second go-round," stated Freeman. "After those two performances we had buyers climbing out of the stands to buy a share; in fact, we sold out in one day."

Although Freeman cut a blind cow in the finals and did not win the Atlantic Coast Futurity, the Smart Little Lena Syndicate had many laurels left to claim. In May, of 1983, Smart Little Lena performed in the NCHA Super Stakes, the second leg of the NCHA Triple Crown. Once again, the stallion won the first go-round, marking a 223, returned to mark a 216.5 in the second go-round, and then a 217 in the semi-finals. In the finals, when Freeman and Smart Little Lena entered the herd seventh in the second bunch of cattle, his closest competitor at the NCHA Futurity, Sugs Gay Lady, led the cutting with a score of 219. Although the arena was tense with suspense, Freeman refused to allow the suspense to penetrate him.

"I wasn't thinking about a score; I was only thinking about getting my horse shown. I knew that was all I could do, the rest was left up to the judges."

Smart Little Lena did his part as well, showing the same style that he demonstrated at the NCHA Futurity, winning the second leg of the Triple Crown with a score of 221 and earning a check for $250,630.90. When questioned about the stallion's uncanny ability, Freeman explained, "He's just a very intelligent horse. He will outthink a cow and can outdo one, too, if he gets in a little bind. He's the best colt I have ridden by far."

With his second victory, Smart Little Lena rapidly became known as the new rising star in the cutting horse industry. Between the Super Stakes and the NCHA Derby, cutting horse enthusiasts flocked to see the stallion at Tommy Manion's ranch in Aubrey, Texas, where the stallion stood. The little runt who had started his cutting career late had become such a legend that a group of investors called the Super Syndicate offered $2.5 million for him. However, since each shareholder would only receive $50,000, the offer was refused. Later, offers of $4 million and of $6 million came from the East Coast, but the intricate details of such a sale could never be finalized. Therefore, Smart Little Lena remained the property of the Smart Little Lena Syndicate.

At the Derby, the final leg of the NCHA Triple Crown, Peppymint Twist ridden by Buster Welch won the first go-round while Taris Catalyst ridden by Dell Bell won the semi-finals. Welch, who drew before Freeman in the Finals, scored a 222.

"I really felt no pressure in the Finals; my horse had already proven himself so it was just a matter of getting him shown to the best of my ability and his," remembered Bill.

Freeman's showmanship and Smart Little Lena's cutting ability once again teamed for a winning score. "The first cow was a good cow; about half treacherous though. However, I wouldn't change anything about that run," stated Freeman. "The second cow allowed the moves that the spectators had become accustomed to seeing."

When the buzzer sounded, Smart Little Lena also received a score of 222, thus becoming Derby Co-Champion with Welch and Peppymint Twist. For his performance, Smart Little Lena earned $59,936.50 and the Triple Crown honor. He had accumulated a total of $577,652.26.

Besides the three NCHA events and the Atlantic Coast Futurity, Smart Little Lena performed at four other shows. He won the first go-round of the 1983 Masters Cutting, and although he lost a cow in the finals, he was the only 4-year-old to advance to the finals. He also won both the Bonanza and the Bonanza Supercut, a cutting limited to champions and reserve champions of other events. Continuing, he won the 1983 Texas Quarter Horse Association Texas Bred Cutting Horse Championship. In 1984, he returned to the Masters Cutting where he once again won the first go-round and this time also claimed the championship. It was in the arena following the Masters finals that Smart Little Lena was officially retired from the cutting arena to the breeding barn. During those eight competitions, he had accumulated earnings of $710,095.36.

Today, Smart Little Lena still spends part of his time at Manion's breeding facilities, breeding mares from February through July. There he resides in the very first stall, constantly surveyed by television monitors and employees during the day, and by monitors and guards during the night. The remainder of the year, he is at home with Freeman, where he is ridden daily and worked occasionally.

Smart Little Lena and Gizmo.

Freeman admits cutting a cow on Smart Little Lena these days is for his own fun as much as for the stallion's.

As of the spring, 1993, Smart Little Lena had sired 755 colts according to the American Quarter Horse Association. 112 of them are AQHA performers and 15 had achieved their Register of Merit. In NCHA competition, according to Equi-Stat, a division of **Quarter Horse News**, 307 offspring had won a total of $7,698,583 since 1987. Also, six of his offspring have won titles in the NCHA Futurity. This is an unprecedented feat for any stallion. Smart Date was the champion in 1987 with Leon Harrel aboard and Smart Little Senor claimed the crown in 1988 with Bill in the saddle. Spencer Harden won 1988 Non-Pro Reserve Champion riding Jazalena. Then, in 1989, Bill rode Commandicate to a reserve championship and in 1990, Terry Riddle claimed reserve with Smart Play. In 1992 Phil Rapp won the Reserve Non-Pro Champion riding Clever Little Lena. Smart Little Lena has the distinction of being the only NCHA Futurity winner sired by an NCHA Futurity winner to also sire an NCHA Futurity winner. And then he went one better; he sired two, and two reserve champions.

The colt who started out as an ugly duckling has left his mark on the cutting horse industry as both a competitor and as a sire. "Smart Little Lena may do a lot down the road for cutting," speculated Freeman. "He has done a lot already and I just went along for the ride. I didn't teach him anything, he taught himself. He himself. He's beautiful inside and out. He's one in a million."

Glossary

Azoturia — a condition in which horses' muscles lock up, particularly the hindquarters. Other symptoms include sweating, pain, and coffee-colored urine. It usually afflicts horses who have been fed high grain rations and are then laid off work for a period of time. Also called Monday Morning Disease because the condition often appears in work horses, who rested on the weekend, and then resumed work on Monday.

Back fence — marked area in the cutting pen behind which the herd is contained by herd holders while the competitor is working. The competitor incurs a penalty should his horse enter this area while working the cow.

Bad-minded — horse that does not accept correction well; a horse that has a bad attitude and resists training.

Bars of the mouth — portion of the horse's lower jaw which is devoid of teeth; space between the tushes (long, pointed teeth) and molars where the bit lies in the mouth.

Big hearted — a horse with exceptional desire to do well. He accepts correction and wants to please his rider.

Breaking pen — round pen used to break colts. Usually has high, solid walls which help prevent the rider from getting injured.

Blister beetle — a type of beetle that invades fields of alfalfa hay. When the hay is harvested with the beetle infestation, horses can die from the ingestion of cantharidin, a poisonous substance secreted by the dead beetles that is toxic to the equine kidney and digestive tract.

Bosal — thick nosepiece made of braided leather; part of a hackamore bridle.

Bumping the bit — pulling lightly on the bit and then releasing to slow the horse down.

Buster Welch bit — a mild bit with a low port that works well on young horses.

Clapper bit — a heavier bit that demands respect from the horse. A good tool for a temperamental or older, soured horse, but one that should not be misused or continually used by the rider.

Conformation — the general shape and size of a horse; the way in which a horse's body is put together.

Control — directing a horse to use his abilities more effectively; maintaining command of the horse without dominating him.

Correctional bit — a curb bit with short shanks and hinged at the cheeks and the mouthpiece; a bit that demands respect but is not as rigid as a solid bit.

Cow interest — a curiosity a horse develops about a cow, demonstrated by his following the movement of a cow with his head; a natural instinct to follow cattle.

Cow-side rein — see direct rein.

Direct rein — direct pressure resulting from a pull on the rein such as when a horse responds to a tug on the right rein by turning right.

Disposition — a horse's attitude towards his handlers and other horses.

Down on the front end — a phrase that refers to a horse shifting his weight to his front end while working a cow.

Drawing — a horse's natural ability to cause the curious cow to move closer to him by the horse's reluctance to step toward the cow.

Dry work — the technique of taking the horse through training maneuvers while the cow is standing still.

Dying in the herd — in a cutting competition the rider "dies in the herd" if the buzzer goes off before the rider has a chance to select another cow to cut.

Ends — that place in a run where the horse stops before he turns around.

Facing up to a cow — when a horse turns his body at a 90° angle with the cow so that he is looking straight at the cow after the cow has stopped, rather than remaining parallel to the cow.

Falling off a cow — the movement, either gradual or immediate, of the horse away from the cow as the two go across the pen. Same as losing ground.

Falling on his head — a term that refers to the manner in which a horse makes a turn incorrectly. He is turning in an unbalanced manner and has allowed all of his weight to be placed on his front end.

False moves — incorrect movements that a horse makes when he anticipates and reacts to a move the cow did or did not make.

Feel — a rhythm between horse and rider.

Flexion — when a horse is made limber throughout his body by a series of exercises designed to make him bend and give to the rider's cues.

Front end — that part of a horse's anatomy that includes the front legs, chest, shoulders, and head of a horse.

Futurity — a competition for horses of a certain age (usually 4 or under) for which entries are made well in advance of the event. As it relates to horse contests, it means a test of a young horse to determine suitability for a particular event.

Give you his head — a horse willingly performing your instructions without resisting you.

Good-minded — a horse that takes correction well, wants to use his mind constructively, and desires to please the rider.

Hackamore — a bitless bridle of Spanish origin (la jaquima) consisting of a simple headstall, bosal or rawhide noseband, heel knot and hair ropes (mecate) used as reins. Pressure points used to control the horse are the nose and jaw.

Heavy on the front end — the act of a horse during a turn that causes all of his weight to be placed on his front end. It can be a conformation problem or a man-made problem.

Herd holders — two riders who are positioned on each side of the herd during a cut and whose responsibility it is to hold the herd behind the cutter after he has selected a cow to work.

Horsemanship — a rider's understanding, like a sixth sense, of what makes a horse tick.

Hot quit — when the horse and rider quit a cow before it is obviously stopped, turned away or behind the turnback horses.

Intensity — a degree of concentration that the horse develops as he matures; a concentrated, intent expression that the horse exhibits while working a cow.

Indirect rein — also called neck-reining. Laying the reins across a horse's neck in the direction you want him to go.

Jointed mouthpiece — mouthpiece of a bit is jointed in the middle, often associated with snaffle bits. Such bits have a nutcracker effect on the horse's jaw.

Leading with the nose — a term used to describe when a horse properly moves into a turn by leading in the direction with his nose first, instead of leading with his shoulder first.

Leaking — drifting toward the cow while working rather than remaining on a level plane. The problem arises when a horse has not completed his stop before a turn.

Leaning on a cow — a horse that angles his body toward the cow as the two cross the pen, applying an almost invisible pressure in an attempt to make the cow run off.

Losing ground — a term referring to a horse moving away from the cow as the two go across the pen. Same as falling off of a cow.

Mechanical horse — a horse who moves only when the rider cues him to move rather than moving with the cow.

National Cutting Horse Association — organization dedicated to the activities of the cutting horse, which approves shows for cutting horse competition, records earnings of cutting horses, and sponsors cutting horse events, such as the NCHA Futurity and Derby.

NCHA Futurity — annual event for 3-year-old horses which have never been shown in cutting competition. Open and non-pro divisions compete each December in Fort Worth, Texas.

Neck-rein — a type of rein response whereby the horse moves away from the pressure of a rein placed against his neck. For example, if the right rein is placed on the right side of the horse's neck, he will move away from the pressure to the left. See also "indirect rein."

Non-professional — a rider who shows in competition but neither professionally trains cutting horses or riders nor receives remuneration for the same.

Over-rotate — a horse's action while working a cow in which he turns more than 180° and, therefore, steps past the point where he should have stopped in his turn.

Plow-rein — see "direct rein."

Pre-futurity works — practice sessions held prior to the NCHA Futurity that simulate the Futurity, offering young horses a chance to become familiar with foreign surroundings.

Pushing with the rib cage — a horse that has extended the rib cage area of his body toward the cow, causing difficulty in turning.

Reading — more intense development of cow interest; a horse that continually pays attention to a cow in an attempt to figure out what the cow is about to do.

Rocking back — the technique of shifting the horse's weight to his hindquarters. This can be accomplished by pulling backwards on both reins with equal force.

Seasoned — a horse that has been hauled away from home and has become accustomed to being in strange surroundings.

Snaffle bit — a bit which exerts pressure on the corners of a horse's mouth. Consists of a jointed or unjointed mouthpiece and O-ring or D-ring cheekpieces. True snaffles have no shanks and, therefore, do not exert leverage on a horse's mouth.

Solo — a horse that works the cow without acknowledgement of the rider.

Sour — cattle that have been worked extensively and, therefore, will either not move or will try to run over the horse.

Stepping across the cow — the technique of a horse changing his body position from having his head parallel with the cow's head to having his head parallel with cow's hip.

Stepping into a cow — moving the horse toward a cow.

Timing — the ability to perform at the precise moment a movement or correction is required.

Too flat — a horse that is at such a parallel position with the cow that it will be difficult for him to turn around smoothly and quickly. The horse will have difficulty controlling the cow in this position.

Too long — when a horse steps past a cow before he stops, creating a space for the cow to return to the herd.

Too short — when a horse does not step out far enough to challenge the cow but rather stays in the areas of the cow's body from the neck to the hip. This allows the cow an opportunity to return to the herd.

Wolf teeth — small teeth that have no function in a horse's mouth. They develop in front of a horse's molars. Pulling them is usually a simple operation and prevents the horse from injuring himself when there is a bit in his mouth.

Appendix A: Competition

There are many opportunities to show cutting horses. The majority of cutting horse contests are sanctioned by the National Cutting Horse Association, the main governing body for cutting competition. The association has two separate programs — aged events and divisional classes.

Aged events are classes restricted according to the horse's age group; i.e. 3-year-old, 4-year-old, 5-year-old, etc. Only horses in a particular age group can compete against other horses in that age group.

Divisional classes usually refer to the competitive status of the rider, such as open, non-pro, limited open, amateur, etc. By far, they are the vast majority of NCHA contests, which take place almost every weekend somewhere in the country. However, divisions are also a part of aged event competition; i.e. 3-year-old open, 4-year-old non-pro, etc.

In aged event competitions, young horses make their first appearance at the end of their 3-year-old year in the prestigious National Cutting Horse Championship Futurity. This aged event provides the largest purse of any cutting competition, usually around $1 million.

Each year thereafter until horses reach the age of six, yearly aged events with big purse stakes— the NCHA Derby for 4-year-olds, the NCHA Classic for 5-year-olds, and the NCHA Challenge for 6-year-olds— offer owners a chance to compete their horses against horses of the same age. All of the NCHA aged events are held in Fort Worth, while aged events hosted by other organizations are held world-wide.

But the aged events are only one part of the cutting horse industry. Scattered throughout the United States and Canada, weekend cuttings with classes that entice greenhorns to professional riders, as well as classes for any age cutting horse attract riders to participate in the sport on a smaller economic scale. The U.S. is divided into 25 NCHA areas providing opportunities for thousands of competitors to win regional awards while accumulating earnings. From these shows, cutters then earn the right to attend the National Finals. Also, those who achieve Top 15 status in the divisional classes earn the right to compete in the World Championship Finals.

According to the NCHA, more than 1,500 of these regional contests are sanctioned every year.

Appendix B: Nutrition

My nutritional program changes with each horse because each one is an individual. I feed horses that are a little hot-blooded (hyper, nervous, etc.) straight oats, bran, and grass hay to help them keep cool, calm, and collected. I rarely give a hot horse vitamin/mineral supplements. For a lazy horse or one that needs more energy, I use a sweet feed, a type that has a high protein content, and grass hay. Usually I will also include a vitamin/mineral mix.

Every horse receives approximately two lids of corn oil in each feeding of grain daily. This promotes a healthy hair coat and keeps the intestines lubricated. We also feed all the horses a vitamin supplement(Clovite) and we add Red Cell for the horses that need a little blood builder.

The feeding program can also change seasonally and it can change for young horses as they grow and mature. In the summertime, I do not feed a high protein feed. It causes too much body heat. Horses fed high levels of protein in hot weather can wash out or fade during performance. And often the excess protein can cause their muscles to lock up. This is called azoturia or Monday Morning Sickness. Some horses can die from this.

Consistency is the key to my program. My horses are fed at 6 a.m. and 6 p.m. everyday. If one is not doing well, I may have it fed hay three or four times a day. Actually, it's best to feed the horse small quantities three or four times a day.

Appendix C: Veterinary Care

When a horse is off, sluggish, or sore, it's a good time to step back and take a close look at him. Examine his hair coat for symptoms of illness. It should not be dull looking. Has the horse lost weight? Have his eyes lost their spark? Is he listless? If such symptoms are noticeable, the first step I take is to call the veterinarian.

I rely heavily on my vet. It is important to have a vet in whom you can put your full trust and who will come at any hour. If you do not have such a relationship with your vet, then I suggest finding another one. The health of your horses depends on it.

All horses 2-years-old and over are tube wormed every three months. The mares, colts, and yearlings are de-wormed every six months.

I have my veterinarian draw blood on my horses every three months to check their blood count. There are several different blood tests that can be used to analyze the blood. When the results are in, I depend on my veterinarian to tell me what I need to do to correct any nutritional problems the horse is having. I step up my vitamin program on those horses with low blood counts.

Dehydration can be a problem, especially for horses that live in hot, humid climates. Check to see if the horse is drinking plenty of water. If he is acting sluggish, ride him enough to break a sweat. If he doesn't, then he might be dehydrated. If this is the case, then most likely his electrolytes are out of balance. In hot weather, I supplement with a lot of electrolytes, which replenish the body with minerals that have been sweated out. The more a horse sweats, the more electrolytes need replenishing. I feed twice the amount of electrolytes that are recommended on the label since what the body does not use are sloughed off anyway. In the winter, I cut back on electrolyte supplementation.

Wolf teeth are a problem, especially with young horses. A wolf tooth is a tooth growing from the gum and not the jaw. It is located in front of the first molar, so a bit or snaffle would strike it when the rider pulls the reins. Therefore, leaving the wolf teeth in would cause the horse a great deal of pain. Unless they are removed, the teeth will grow down and possibly lacerate a horse's gums. Obviously, this type of pain can interfere with a horse's performance.

Some horses don't grow any wolf teeth at all and some grow just one. But no matter how many there are, I have them extracted. I check for wolf teeth periodically. There is no set time that wolf teeth come in, but generally they show up half way through the horse's two-year-old year.

One way a horse can tell you if he is physically hurting is when he pops his tail (lifts his tail sharply). Tail popping can mean that he is hurting in his hindquarter or in his back. However, I have seen horses pop their tails when they were hurting other places, also. It could just be soreness and the solution might be a few days rest. If this does not help, then I immediately have him checked by the vet and the chiropractor.

A mare that is tail popping might be doing so because her ovaries hurt. A few days of rest may solve the problem. If not, she needs to be palpated to make sure there is no medical problem, such as enlarged ovaries or a cyst on the ovaries.

Appendix D: Chiropractic Care

My interest in chiropractic therapy began back in the mid eighties. My dad had been using Graeme Boyd, an equine chiropractor, for quite some time. Whenever Daddy encouraged me to try a chiropractor, I laughed at the idea and called it voodoo medicine.

One day the two of them showed up unannounced at my barn. My dad suggested I let Boyd look at my horses. At the time I was having problems with a gelding I was riding for Daddy. I decided I had nothing to lose and pointed to the gelding in its stall.

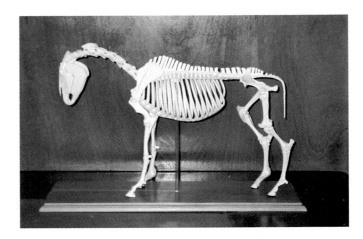

I offered no comment about the problems I was having. Boyd put his hands on the accupressure points of the horse and, to my surprise, he knew the problem exactly. He said I was having problems with the horse turning around. I had always credited myself as being a horseman but the ability of this man to tell me the specific problem in my training program just by a touch amazed me. A hit on the pressure point with one finger made the adjustment and relieved the horse's pain.

Many times since then Boyd has told me the exact problem I was having with a horse in my training program. Now I have Boyd check all the horses in my barn every three months. Through feel, pressure points, and observation of how a horse carries himself, he can locate problem areas of misalignment.

For example, if a horse does not want to follow my lead through a turn and starts carrying his head off to one side, it might mean that his neck is out of alignment. With this problem, the horse cannot turn correctly; and since he is experiencing pain, his mind is not totally on the training program.

Often Boyd's expertise has helped me succeed at numerous shows. One time I was having trouble with a mare at a major event. Her moves were not flowing but rather very stiff. We just barely got through the go-rounds. Yet after Boyd adjusted her, she was totally relaxed. It was like riding a different horse. We made the finals and I seriously doubt that we would have without chiropractic treatment.

High Brow Hickory is another horse which was helped by chiropractic care. At the pre-futurity works before the NCHA Futurity, he was not turning to the right as well as he usually did. Although his turn looked alright to several other cutters, it did not feel right to me. After the chiropractor adjusted him, I immediately noticed a definite improvement. High Brow Hickory performed so well that we won the NCHA Futurity Reserve Championship.

Although I have become a strong advocate of chriropractor care for horses, I don't believe every horse needs chiropractic care. And it is certainly not a substitute for medical care. If I run into a problem in my training program, I always call the vet first. Then if I feel the chiropractor can help, I will give him a call.

Index

Credits

Many thanks to the National Cutting Horse Association for permission to reprint the penalties that can be incurred while showing a cutting horse.

All pictures in this book were photographed by Kathy Kadash and Rick Swan with the exception of the following pages:

15	Dalco Film Company
42	Jim Bortvedt
148	Danny Huey Photography
149	Pat Hall Photography
152	Pat Hall Photography
154-155	Don Shugart Photography
158	Pat Hall Photography
162-163	Don Shugart Photography
166	Don Shugart Photography
170-171	Quarter Horse Journal
172	Karen Freeman
173	Dalco Film Company
174	Pat Hall Photography
183	Graeme Boyd